ARISTOTLE'S PSYCHOLOGY

Daniel N. Robinson

ARISTOTLE'S PSYCHOLOGY

Columbia University Press
NEW YORK

Columbia University Press
New York   Oxford
Copyright © 1989 Columbia University Press
All rights reserved

LIbrary of Congress Cataloging-in-Publication Data

Robinson, Daniel N., 1937–
Aristotle's psychology / Daniel N. Robinson.
    p.   cm.
Bibliography: p
Includes index.
ISBN 0-231-07002-0
1. Aristotle—Contributions in psychology.
2. Psychology—History.
I. Title.
B491.P8R6   1989
150.ppra.92—dc20
89-32235
CIP

Printed in the United States of America

Casebound editions of Columbia University Press books are Smyth-sewn
and printed on permanent and durable acid-free paper

FOR FRANCINE

Ginoito d' an kai askesis tis tes
aretes ek tou suzen tois agathois,
kathaper kai Theognis phesin.

Nicomachean Ethics, 1170^a 11–13

CONTENTS

PREFACE

Aristotle's contributions over the widest range of subjects are often so original and insightful that he has tended to be treated as a contemporary in every age of scholarship; to such an extent that philosophical and scientific reputations have been made over the centuries by corrections and qualifications of works composed by Aristotle a thousand or two thousand years earlier. Any attempt, therefore, to compress his wide-ranging and deeply informed Psychology into a book of manageable length and accessible to the nonspecialist is doomed at the outset. One hopes only to fail well!

The task is further complicated by the scattered distribution of Aristotle's writings on the subject. Consider only the cogent discussion of the emotions in his *Rhetoric* and the principles governing behavior at a choice-point examined in *Topics*. Examples could be multiplied. Aristotle's Psychology appears in his logical treatises, his ethical and political writings, his scientific and ethological works. Against this background, *On the Soul*—the treatise most frequently consulted in this connection—is actually more on the order of an outline than a detailed exposition of his developed Psychology.

Of this Psychology, it is safe to say that it is history's first fully integrated and systematic account and, to some extent, the one that remains the most complete. Directly and indirectly it has been among the most influential as well. Within the surviving works can be found theories of learning and memory, perception, motivation and emotion, socialization, personality. The theories address these from both a biogenetic and an environmental perspective, usually enriched by discerning comparisons between and among species and by a nearly modern respect for the more important factors influencing the development of habitual modes of adaptation. When *human* psychology comes under scrutiny great complexities are introduced, and Aristotle faces them squarely. The powers of rationality yield such creations as ethics, law, and the *polis* itself; creations unheralded by the balance of nature and calling for modes of analysis and explanation beyond those of the natural scientist. To his other accomplishments, then, can be added those of the methodologist and philosopher of science. His reach and range are without parallel. Accordingly, overly confident summaries of his work are often embarrassed by the texts themselves, whereas the better scholarship can prove to be irksomely, if pardonably, equivocal.

It should be noted in this connection that the very term "psychology" presents difficulties in its own right. The studies that become significant for Aristotle as a result of *psyche* go far beyond the topics filling today's psychology texts. And, in the matter of these latter topics, we see that he found it necessary to qualify an otherwise uncompromising naturalism, a *psych*-ology. For Aristotle the naturalist, digestion is no less "psychic" than perception or memory; but for Aristotle the psychologist, human rationality is unlike digestion or perception or any other process that can be explained physiologically.

Aristotle was, of course, the rarest of geniuses. He had great teachers, however, and was the citizen of a great, if already declining, civilization. The problems he set out to solve are no less "Hellenic" for being ageless. They were dealt with before Aristotle, not only by his illustrious mentor but also by the poets, dramatists, and sages of the ancient Greek world. The first two chapters present an outline of these contextual influences. These two chapters are little more than summaries of material well-known to students of ancient history and thus need not be consulted by them. For readers less familiar with the ancient Greek world and with the principal teachings of the Socratic-Platonic school, chapters 1 and 2 will be useful. Although Aristotle is still remarkably "contemporary" in so many respects, he nonetheless remains the citizen of a remote epoch and a unique culture.

A few concluding words must be reserved to acknowledge the daunting and inevitable problems created by translations. They make every interpretation possible, but they also hold every interpretation hostage. My own limited powers with classical Greek are exercised only occasionally in the following pages, chiefly where it becomes useful to compare Aristotle's own direct and economical (if sometimes severe) prose with an otherwise authoritative English rendition. Fortunately, recent decades have yielded a small library of Aristotle scholarship of a very high order. The present work relies heavily on it and strives to do it justice. But there are still unavoidable differences in the interpretation of Aristotle's subtle and sometimes inconsistent treatises. The more important of these differences are noted and briefly discussed in the notes to each chapter.

ARISTOTLE'S PSYCHOLOGY

ONE

The Ancient Greek Context

As Plato composed his dialogues, the Homeridae stood up to defend the ageless orthodoxies of the Greek people. It was these "sons of Homer" who insisted that all historical, religious, and scientific knowledge was to be found in the epic poems of Homer, and that departure from these was heresy and dangerous folly. The appearance of the Homeridae marks an important point in the development of ancient Greek culture; the point at which philosophical modes of inquiry had come to provide formidable challenges to those ageless certainties on which Greek civilization had been erected. Like Plato himself, the Homeridae found in the waste and rubble of the Peloponnesian wars the clearest evidence of moral waywardness. Men had turned their backs on those ideals of perfection personified in the Age of Heroes and rhapsodized centuries later by the blind poet whose name means "hostage." But unlike Plato, who sought to devise a political regime according to the discoveries of a critical philosophy, the Homeridae proposed a return to what was a mythic past, though one still alive in the Hellenic imagination. It is this past that supplied the Hellenes with their folk-psychology and an overarching conventional wisdom that would first test and, finally, rise up against the new philosphy.[1]

G. Lowes Dickinson observed nearly a century ago,[2] that the ancient Greeks had fashioned a religion that might make them more at home in the world by making the world and even themselves less mysterious and terrifying. The Homeric epics provide the most complete depiction of this extraordinary invention and of the nature of the relationship between gods and men. Long after *Iliad* and *Odyssey* had come to be recognized as essentially poetical reconstructions of history, the Hellenic perspective was still "Homeric" in its daily and unphilosophical operations. And, where there were significant departures from the Homeric perspective, these were in the direction of ever darker mysteries.[3]

As early as the time of Hesiod, Homer's near contemporary, a voice is given to the fear that mankind had so degenerated as to cause the gods themselves to turn away. In *The Works and Days*, Hesiod laments that "fifth generation" of men created by Zeus of the wide brows; Hesiod's own generation, those of the Age of Iron. This is a degraded species, destined to be ruled by envy, shameless in the sight of the gods. Thus,

> The vile man will crowd his better out, and attack him . . .
> and at last Nemesis and Aidos, Decency and
> Respect, shrouding their bright forms in
> pale mantles, shall go from the wide-wayed earth,
> Back on their way to Olympos, forsaking the whole race
> of mortal men . . .
> And there shall be no defense against evil.[4]

1. Commenting on this general theme, Cornford observed that, "All ancient thought is haunted by regret for a golden age in the remote past and by the hope that the reign of Cronos will some day return." F. M. Cornford, *The Unwritten Philosophy* p. 45 in the edition of 1967. It is important, however, not to confuse this with nostalgia or paralyzing resignation. Even as it was haunted by a species of regret, ancient thought also actively pursued perfection and took the bygone age of the Heroes as something that *could* be brought about, because it *had* been brought about.

2. G. Lowes Dickinson, *The Greek View of Life*. The seventeenth edition (1932) is referred to here. Perhaps this classic treatise overstates matters when it describes the ancient Greek as one who "lived and acted undisturbed by scrupulous introspection; and the function of his religion was rather to quiet the conscience by ritual than to excite it by admonition and reproof" (p. 66). There is, after all, more than a little admonition and reproof in Hesiod, Pindar, Aeschylus, Euripedes, and (even) Aristophanes. But the austerity of ancient religion never reached the *unnaturalness* of Puritan Christianity, for example, or the exotic mythologies of Asiatic beliefs.

3. One need only compare the essentials of Olympianism with, for example, the Eleusinian Mysteries, Orphism, Dionysianism, or what we assume to be true of the more fervent Pythagoreans.

4. Hesiod's *The Works and Days*, Fr. 265. The eighth edition (1973) is used here.

If there is one characteristic of the ancient Greek achievement in all of its variety and richness, it is this impulse to externalize the entire panoply of fears, beliefs, values and aspirations that animated Hellenic civilization. In this regard, the art and architecture, poetry and drama, philosophy and science of the Greeks are expressions of a pervasive spirit, a commanding and ordering cast of mind whose integrity is as apparent in the wars among the Hellenes as in their cooperative ventures. This impulse is of course one of the sources of philosophy itself, and especially that body of ethical and social philosophy created by Socrates and his disciples. But even before such academic pursuits appeared in Greece, the religion of the place, its Olympianism, had yielded the external forms of the popular consciousness.

What can be said of this consciousness is that it took for granted an intended order in the affairs of man and nature, and regarded deviations from this with the gravest concern. In this, there is not the undeliberated allegiance to mere custom, but the seeds of a metaphysical system that promises woeful consequences to those who scorn the will of the gods or invite their envy.

A single example helps make the point clearer. Consider the "causes" of the Trojan War. One account finds Priam ordering the murder of his infant son whose birth threatens to fulfill what has been portended in Hecuba's dream; viz., that the fire emerging from her body will destroy the entire state. But Priam's command is not obeyed, and the infant is left to the elements on Mt. Ida, only to survive and prosper among the peasants. His gallantry and virtues become widely known. But next, there occurs the marriage of Peleus and Thetis, the former a (mere) mortal has imposed himself on a goddess. All attend the great event, but the goddess Discordia has been overlooked and she, ever resentful, drops in the midst of the throng a golden apple bearing the inscription, "For the most beautiful." Juno, Minerva, and Venus are the finalists, and, alas, Priam's long-orphaned son, Paris, is asked to choose the winner. Each contestant promises favor; distinction in battle from Minerva, riches from Juno, and, from Venus, marriage to the world's most beautiful woman. Paris chooses Venus and thus makes his subsequent abduction of Helen inevitable.

But what, then, is *the* cause of the Trojan War? Is it a reprisal against Priam for the attempted infanticide? Or are the Fates fulfilling the prophesy recorded in the dream of Hecuba? Is it the dreadful punishment occasioned by that display of hubris that would have a mortal betrothed to a god? And this is only the account from the Trojan side of the dispute. There is also the curse on the house of King Atreus, one of whose sons, Menelaus, has lost Helen to Paris while the other, Agamemnon, will ultimately die at the hands of his own wife. Does Agamemnon go forth solely to avenge the abduction of Helen? Is he, instead, impelled by destinies beyond his reach and ken? He embitters his greatest warrior, Achilles (the offspring of Peleus and Thetis), even before the ships sail for Troy, refusing to relinquish the captive daughter of one of Apollo's favorite priests. But is the lesson, then, never to invite the wrath of a god? Or has this episode displayed only that grudging and overly proud side of Agamemnon that will lead him to sacrifice his own innocent daughter and thus turn Clytemnestra into a faithless wife and mortal enemy?

It is part of the timelessness of Homer's epics that such questions are never answered firmly or finally. Nonetheless, it is in the same epics that an inchoate theory of mind and spirit finds its earliest expression in Greek civilization. Throughout Homer's works a prescientific terminology is invoked to explain the actions of men and gods. The dream-demon sent by Zeus works on the psyche of the dreamer, but there are many other modes of psychological function that do not depend upon psyche. More often than not, the waking soul, or the aspect of it that impels the actor to action, is rendered as *thymos*, and is typically located in the chest.[5] It is the *thymos*, for example, that pities the fallen Trojans. Then, too, there is always the *noos* (later *nous*) of the gods to contend with, and the protentous reminder that Zeus's *noos* must forever outstrip that of mortals. The term here refers to a rational plan or intended outcome, a strategy whose implementation requires certain mortals to face specific challenges. And then there is *menos*, the noble fury that overtakes the hero and drives him toward death and glory. There is no valor without *menos*. But an even greater insinuation can cause a man to reach an utterly heedless fury once he is possessed by *lyssa*. As Jan Bremmer has written:

> [I]n Homer the equivalent of the berserk's fury is expressed by the word *lyssa*, or "wolf's rage," as appears from the words of

5. Sustained scholarship, beginning with Erwin Rohde's monumental *Psyche* (1894), has been devoted to the ancient Greek conception of the soul. A balanced and accessible review of this literature, combined with original and informing scholarship of its own, will be found in Jan Bremmer's *The Early Greek Concept of the Soul*.

Odysseus when he describes Hector: "Hector, exulting greatly in his might, rages vehemently, relying on Zeus and holding no one in respect, neither men nor gods. And the powerful *lyssa* has entered him." A warrior possessed by the *lyssa* . . . had stopped being fully human.[6]

In every place in which Homer supplies any sort of efficient cause to explain the behavior or the dispositions of his principal characters, the work of the soul is closely fastened to body; often it is a modification of the body or even some colorless breath emanating from it. Homer does not entirely naturalize *psyche* but, like Aristotle centuries later, he seldom permits it to wander beyond the sublunary realms of enmattered things!

The destruction of Troy—the Troy of Homer's epic—occurred at about 1250 b.c., perhaps four or five centuries before the poet composed his immortal song. It is doubtful that anyone in the Hellenic Age, even the most faithful of the Homeridae, believed any of these legendary accounts, chapter and verse. Indeed, in the *Acharnians*, Aristophanes spoofs the whole affair in a passage that finds the world ablaze because of three whores![7] But the question of credulity is quite beside the point, for the influence of the epics was not academic or scholarly. It is not to be estimated in terms of the willingness of later ages to accept its historicity. Rather, in the *Iliad* and *Odyssey*, Homer has given solidity to the very concept of virtue. Through these works, the ideals of virtue and justice and decency have been externalized in living and memorable form. The long and irresistible arm of fate and the dispository powers of the gods have been indelibly recorded in the mind of an age. The complexities of the human condition, the frailties and foibles even of great men—even of the gods—have been given a name and a story. And an enduring lesson has been taught: There can be no certainties, but the greatest chance for a good and prosperous life

6. Bremmer, p. 59.
7. The Old Comedy of ancient Greece is a breed apart, even by the liberated standards of theater. As Nathan Dane and John Ambrose observe, "All contemporary matters and all contemporary figures were fair targets for the libelous and cutting thrusts of the comedian. Nothing was inviolate." In Nathan Dane and John Ambrose, eds., *Greek Attitudes*, (New York: Scribner, 1974), p. 320. As for the real causes of the war between the Achaeans and the Trojans—or if there really was one of the sort depicted in the epics—theories abound and the theorists have things pretty much their own way. The settled view at present is that there were probably many skirmishes, large and small, between these peoples, based chiefly on competition for trade routes. Still informative on this and related questions is Martin P. Nilsson, *Homer and Mycenae*.

awaits him who does his duty, respects the law, and strives to conform his own powers to those Olympian models who, at their very best, are perfection itself.

Every human passion is in evidence in the lives and mixed fortunes of Homer's gods and heroic figures. Every human potentiality is realized, as are the wages of weakness and corruption. The stories are at once a theory of human nature and the backdrop against which competing theories might seek support. Surrounding the whole, as a kind of disembodied intelligence, is the spirit of law, *Nomos*, which sets the limits and judges the true value of every act and actor. In *The Eumenides*, the finale of Aeschylus' somber trilogy, the trial of Orestes is conducted in Athens, the counsel for the defense being none other than Apollo, with Athene herself there to guide the Athenians toward a just verdict. "Do not taint pure laws with new expediency," she tells them, and she goes on to remind them that their fortunes are the gift of law.[8] Here is the patron-goddess of Athens, telling the faithful that theirs is the city where the gods most love to live because of its great beauty; Athene, honored with a forty-foot statue, perhaps the most wonderful ever made, placed prominently within the Acropolis which, itself, is the outward sign of a devotion to the idea of perfection. The same theme is developed even more insistently in Hesiod's *Works and Days* (Fragment 256 ff.) where the chief interest of Zeus is personified in the maiden Justice, "the daughter of Zeus glorified and honored by the gods."

In the fall of 490 B.C., Athenian forces won the decisive victory at marathon and put to rest the theory of the invincibility of the "Medes." Persia attempted to enslave the people of Athens for the support they had given to the rebellious Greeks of Ionia, whose several settlements hosted the first great advances in Greek (pre-Socratic) philosophy. The glory of Marathon was Athens' own, in this case the Spartan forces arriving too late. But the effect of the victory was general. Throughout mainland Greece there was a surge of artistic and intellectual energy inspired by accomplishments of nearly Homeric proportions. Herodotus estimates, probably correctly, that 6,400 Persians lost their lives, but less than 200

---

8. But Athene in *The Eumenides* also puts the Chorus on notice when she tells them that they call on Justice whereas she consults Zeus—and has the key that gives access to his thunderbolts! Aeschylus in this gives voice to both senses of *dike;* the developed sense of *justice,* and the original sense of "the path chosen by the gods."

Greeks.[9] Heroes and villains abounded and virtue triumphed. Athens learned of the victory in less than three hours, the good news delivered by brave and devoted Pheidippides, who raced the twenty-two mile course, his life giving out near the entrance to the city.

A nearly contrapuntal relationship existed between the Homeric ideals and the actual history of the ancient Greek world. With the Persian threat now diminished, the Greeks could return to their celebrated preoccupation of warring among themselves. Like their gods, they were easily insulted and given to spiteful excesses. Their political fortunes oscillated between aristocracies leaning toward tyranny and democracies tending toward anarchy. In this small world of "first families," factionalism was of an almost hereditary character. Solon had outlawed *phratric justice* in the sixth century, but the blood feuds escalated from the level of the tribe to that of entire city-states.

This part of Greek history reveals a side of the Hellenes otherwise concealed in those remnants of the foundations of Western civilization. They were a superstitious, proud, and often erratic people, suspicious of others and generally hostile toward innovation. It must not be forgotten that the age that was able to produce Socrates was also prepared to execute him. The stern moral lessons taught by Aeschylus would have been received as empty truisms were they widely and uncritically adopted in the daily life of Athenians. Instead, Aeschylus was revered for seeing more clearly than others the special and divinely forged bond that ties a man's destiny to his character. A century or so later, a restored Athenian democracy (403 B.C.) will conveniently find Socratic teaching a threat to those very traditions exalted by Aeschylus. A confused and wary populace will not let the life of one good man disturb the hard-won order of the city.

But even with their worst nature exposed under the often harsh light of history, the ancient Greeks did achieve that extraordinary synthesis of ethics, aesthetics, and politics which was not to be attained again, and only rarely attempted. The synthesis arose

9. Herodotus gives this estimate in Book VI, Sec. 117, of his *Persian Wars*. George Rawlinson notes that the Persians probably fielded a force of some 15,000. A battle in which the losing side suffers 40 percent fatalities would involve sustained hand-to-hand combat, combat at such close quarters as to prevent orderly retreat. If this was the case, then the Greek losses, alleged by Herodotus to be 192, cannot be explained in terms of superior generalship or strategy. The edition of Herodotus consulted is Herodotus, *The Persian Wars*, translated by George Rawlinson, in *The Greek Historians*. Francis R. B. Godolphin, ed.

from an idea that was new to the world, the idea that beauty is one face of truth, and that moral goodness is itself a species of the beautiful. Instances are numerous in the prose and poetry of the Hellenic world, as well as in the philosophical treatises, of persons described as beautiful *because* of their characters, and of statesmen accepted as virtuous *because* of the art and architecture they supported. This will all come to be an integral feature of Aristotle's own theory of human nature. Nor is it to be confused with well-known passages in Plato's dialogues in which the need for early exposure to fine art is underscored.[10] In these matters, Plato is perhaps least original, for the broad foundations of this perspective were already centuries old before Socrates and his friends assembled. The foundations are Homeric and when, in the fourth century B.C., they began to crack and crumble, Greek civilization itself began its slide toward oblivion.

It is easy to speak of a synthesis of ethics, aesthetics, and politics, but a far from easy phenomenon to comprehend now more than twenty centuries after the fact. If it is to be understood, it is necessary to begin with an observation that might seem surprising and certainly not readily validated. Between roughly the ninth and sixth centuries B.C., on the Greek mainland and in the Greek colonies of Asia Minor and Magna Graecia, it became possible for the most authentic and enduring aspects of human nature to flourish. Guided by a religious imagination that would, nonetheless, never produce a theology, the Hellenes constructed a pantheon of models designed to represent their own most ardent aspirations. In the process, they disclosed these very aspirations, such that the entire age is something of a collective *Confessions* and a strikingly candid one at that. Acted out at the safe distance of the Olympian theater, the innermost lives of the Hellenes were made boldly clear; their dreams of power, their nightmares, their conceptions of themselves and others.

10. The arts in Plato, and perhaps even more so in Aristotle, are emblematic and are tied to the notion of *harmonia*. But *haromina* itself is only latterly a musical attribute. Its pristine meaning is closer to *fitting* or *apt*. Pieces of a puzzle achieve *harmonia* when they all fit easily together and yield collectively what never would have been suspected on viewing any one or several of them. The conviction central to ancient Greek thought is that *harmonia* lies behind all the perceived order of the cosmos and is expressed in the very best human productions. Commenting on Pythagoras's famous study of the musical scale, Cornford says, "Pythagoras would never have made the experiment, if he had not already divined that the order and beauty evoked by the art of music . . . might be reducible to the pure abstractions of number" (p. 19).

To say that the most authentic and enduring aspects of human nature flourished is, of course, to take something of a settled position on the nature of human nature, and this is precarious to say the least. But recorded human history, and the significant aspects of each individual life are colored by themes and tensions, passions and prospects so ubiquitous as to be regarded as universal. Just these themes, tensions, passions, and prospects are central to Hellenic literature and speculation. What flourished, then, in the Hellenic world were the seemingly universal forms of human thought and sentiment; forms initially embodied in legendary figures, but finally translated into the subject matter that comprises philosophy and science. What begins with Homer as a story, leads first to the devotional and celebratory liturgy of the ancient religion, often Dionysian. But out of the provincialism of ritual arises the ancient Greek drama, now liberated from time and place and able to enlighten the ages. And then, just after Aeschylus (525–455 B.C.) and Sophocles (495–405 B.C.) have literally *set the stage*, Socrates (469?–399 B.C.) replaces the didactic morality play of the dramatist with the *dialectical* science of the moral philosopher. By and large, however, the content would remain constant from the time of Homer. It has remained constant, in important respects, to the present.

The Homeric world view was ubiquitous, but it was not hegemonous, and both skeptical and mystical views would gain force and popularity in the wake of the Peloponnesian war. The plays of Euripedes (480–406 B.C.), with their open scorn of Apollo (viewed as having aided the Spartans at the expense of Athens), mark the passing of a more innocent age. In *Ion*, Euripedes dramatizes what had become a matter of great popular concern; viz, the credibility of the Oracles and the trustworthiness of the gods themselves. Not only does Apollo perform as a brutal rapist and liar in the play, but he goes so far as to have the Pythia of Delphi aid him in his deceptions. The message is clear: Can *anything* be believed with confidence? How long must Athens remain a hostage to superstition and habit?

Then, too, there were competing religious outlooks fervently embraced and widely distributed in the Hellenic sphere of influence. Their importance arises less from their popularity—in the main, they were regarded as odd sects even in their own time—than from the light they shed on the evolution of early philosophy. Chief among these was *Orphism* which appeared in the ancient

world during the sixth and fifth centuries B.C.[11] The precise origins
of this cult or religion are not known, though the Greek colony of
Crotona on Italy's east coast was a major setting for its development. Crotona, of course, was to be the setting also for Pythagoras'
political and intellectual attainments, and for the formation of his
sect of devoted followers.[12] Even the principal teachings of Orphism are difficult to specify, and must be patched together from
passages in Plato, from fragments attributable to Empedocles, and
from the vagrant comments of one or another later commentator.
That it was a religion of sin and redemption there is no doubt, and
that it promised a life for the soul beyond the grave is also clear. In
these respects, it is utterly at variance with Homeric and Hesiodic
teachings. But there are other heresies as well. The Orphics taught
that the soul predates the body and, through sin, becomes locked
in this prison house *(desmoterion)*, far removed from the gods with
whom it had shared company. What is longed for is liberation and
deliverance, a return to the abode of the divine, a purification and
transcendence.

But Orphism is not an anticipation of Christianity so much as a
version of more primitive Eastern beliefs in multiple incarnations,
great cycles of degradation and redemption, a scepticism toward
the reality of earthly life. It is the otherworldly element in Greek
thought; the element that will animate much of the religious spirit
of the Platonic dialogues and will even reveal itself in the Aristotle
of the *Protrepticus*.[13] In his *Purifications*, Empedocles escapes the
bonds of humanity and rises to the level of the immortals. The
Socratic account is more detailed:

> For every soul of man has in the way of nature beheld true being;
> this was the condition of her passing into the form of man. But
> all souls do not easily recall the things of the other world . . . For

11. Still informing is James Adam's *The Religious Teachers of Greece*, the Gifford Lectures published in 1908. A recent edition has been published by Reference Book Publishers.
Lecture 5 "Orphic Religious Ideas," establishes Orphic connections between Hesiodic and
Platonic views, even while noting Plato's often harsh rebukes of Orphism.
12. The cultural war between Sybaris and Crotona—which would culminate in naval
blockades!—is but another instance of the seriousness with which ancient Greeks ap-
proached questions of orthodoxy. This would seem peculiar in light of the rather thin
"theology" of the epoch. But Dickinson saw right through the apparent contradiction when
he wrote of "the ideal of that marvellous corporate life where there is no ecclesiastical
religion only because there was no secular state" (p. 11).
13. There will be occasion in later chapters to examine various "genetic" theories of
Aristotle's intellectual life and the extent to which a work such as the *Protrepticus* might be
regarded either as central to his entire program or the legacy of a Platonism he came to
abandon.

10

there is no clear light of justice or temperance, or any of the
higher ideas which are precious to souls, in the earthly copies of
them; they are seen through a glass dimly. . . . There was a time
when, with the rest of the happy band, they saw beauty shining
in brightness—we philosophers following in the train of Zeus,
others in company with other gods; and then we beheld the
beatific vision and were initiated into a mystery which may be
truly called most blessed . . . pure ourselves and not yet en-
shrined in that living tomb which we carry about, now that we
are imprisoned in the body, and like the oyster in his shell. Let
me linger over the memory of scenes which have passed away.
(*Phaedrus* 249ᵈ)[14]

Like the *ekstasis* of the Dionysiac revellers, Orphic liberation is
a movement of the spirit out of the body whereupon it resumes a
daemonic existence of a godlike nature.[15] The result is more than
an intimation of immortality! As James Adam wrote,

The nerveless, shadowy phantom which Homer called the soul is
beginning to disappear, and in its place we have a divine ethereal
essence, by the side of which the perishable body is of compara-
tively slight account. The Orphic doctrine of the divinity of the
soul not only introduces a new and more spiritual conception
both of God and man; it also provides a basis for the belief in
immortality.[16]

In later chapters, it will be noted that Aristotle's position on the
so-called "mind-body problem" was finally dualistic, and that he
regarded at least the rational aspect of the human psyche as imperishable. He does not arrive at this position through anything as
crude and untested as Orphism, but Orphic teachings do reflect a
movement away from that very Olympianism that would also con-
demn Aristotle's conclusions.

The longing for immortality is found as well outside the pre-
cincts of Orphic belief. The *Eleusinian Mysteries*, for example—

14. Translation by Benjamin Jowett, taken from *The Dialogues of Plato* in two volumes.
15. Dionysos is ever obscure. He was a god of the Thracians whose pedigree and
gestation were remarkable, to say the least. The legend finds Zeus attracted to mortal
Semele, daughter of mortal Cadmus. Jealous Hera gets Zeus to appear before Semele in his
full godliness, and she perishes. Her fetus is rescued from the ashes and completes his
development within the thigh of Zeus. The saga of Dionysos thus begins and will retain
exotic features down through the ages, usually including revellers, mad women, drunks,
and other doubtful types in the retinue. They follow the god, or man-god, hopeful of
attaining that state of *enthusiasmos* which frees them from earthly bondage.
16. Adam, *Religious Teachers*.

presided over by Demeter and Kore—are celebrated in the so-called "Homeric Hymns" and provide inspiration for the devotional poetry of Pindar. It is not clear just what the Eleusinian initiates were taught, or even what the formal rites were, though the entire Greek world contained pockets of the faithful in this and in still other cults. In this, there is evidence that the Greek mind was not fully appeased by Homeric epics and Hesiodic calls to duty. Homer had made the gods familiar. Orphic and Eleusinian teachings made them *familial*.

The line between the familiar and the familial is not always wide or vivid. If Orphism boldly declared man to be in the image of the divine and in possession of an immortal soul, so too did the religion of Homer declare the Olympians to be similar to mankind in any number of respects, and even occasionally hostage to earthly charms. Thus, the full range of ancient Greek religious sentiment has anthropomorphic underpinnings, whether the prevailing sentiment is one of duty, or of hope, or of contrition. And so, too, does the ancient Greek conscience arrange itself around considerations of imperfection and of *sin* as a failure to come up to the expectations of the gods. This consideration of imperfection is apparent in the Homeric and Hesiodic attention to duty and justice, but equally in the Orphic concern with the soul's redemption. Across the entire range of beliefs and at the center of the most influential myths, there is a unifying concept that puts an identifying stamp on all of the major productions of the epoch. It is the concept of *character*, and it will come to be the chief preoccupation of Socrates and of Aristotle after him. It is this concept that comes to attract and absorb the religious and poetic ideals of justice, beauty, and the divine, itself.

TWO

The Socratic Context

Aristotle devoted nearly twenty years of his life, first to an eager but inevitably to a reluctant discipleship in Plato's Academy. This school and its famous teacher establish the broad intellectual context within which Aristotle's own ideas took shape and from which they would depart in truly revolutionary ways. The relationship between Aristotle and this school was complex and has resisted numerous attempts at illumination. Marjorie Grene, a quarter of century ago, summarized scholarship on this question in a way that remains apt:

> Those who are steeped in the dialectic of the Platonic dialogues, for whom western thought is a "series of footnotes to Plato," see in Aristotle a pupil who misconstrued his master. . . . Those more interested in the development of logic . . . are inclined to see in Plato's work a first adumbration of a correct logic, brought to full flower by his most brilliant pupil. . . . [T]here are also, scattered through the literature, proponents of a third view, which respects equally both master and pupil, but sees in the relation between them neither essential decline nor essential progress,

but two deeply divergent attitudes to experience, to man and the world.[1]

It is the third view that Marjorie Grene adopts and that is adopted here as well. But just what were these Platonic or Socratic "attitudes to experience, to man and the world"? And was Aristotle's divergence of attitude so great as to remove his most basic intellectual impulses from the domain in which they were given their earliest nurturance and direction?

As the passage from the *Phaedrus* quoted in chapter 1 illustrates, Socrates is nostalgic for the age of heroes and, for all of his philosophical intensity, still takes Homer for his guide. Examples are numerous, but one from the *Apology* is sufficient. In cross-examining Socrates, Meletus has made clear that the death penalty hangs in the balance. Socrates replies that the good man fears disgrace, not death, and chides Meletus thus:

> Whereas, upon your view, the heroes who fell at Troy were not good for much, and the son of Thetis above all, who altogether despised danger in comparison with disgrace; and when he was so eager to slay Hector, his goddess mother said to him, that if he avenged his companion Patroclus, and slew Hector, he would die himself—"Fate", she said, in these or the like words, "waits for you next after Hector"; he, receiving this warning, utterly despised danger and death, and instead of fearing them, feared rather to live in dishonour. (*Apology* 28)[2]

The distinct identities of Socrates and Plato have not surrendered their secrets, but Socrates is clearly a child of Homer in a way that Plato would have found, and did find, innocent if endearing. Neither Xenophon nor Plato credits Socrates with a formal theological system, though Plato, in the words of J. Burnet, "has left us the first systematic defence of Theism we know of" (p. 81).[3] The Socratic context, then, is not quite the same as the Platonic, and the Academy of Aristotle's schooldays has already moved a distance from the one presided over by Socrates himself.

Brief attempts to establish "the" Socratic context must be hazardous and less than successful. The philosophical Socrates is known

1. Marjorie Grene, *A Portrait of Aristotle*, pp. 38–41.
2. This and all other passages from the dialogues are taken from *The Dialogues of Plato*, translated by Benjamin Jowett and published in two volumes by Random House. Standard enumerations are given in the text.
3. J. Burnet, "Philosophy," in R. W. Livingstone, ed., *The Legacy of Greece*.

most fully through Plato's dialogues, but these were composed over a course of many years and reflect quite substantial changes in Plato's methods and perspective. It appears that the last of his major works was the *Laws*, not completed at the time of his death (347 B.C.) and separated from Socrates' execution (399 B.C.) by more than a half-century.

Scholarship has identified three different periods in Plato's philosophical development. The first period included the years when Socrates was still alive and able to exert a direct and personal influence on several of the earliest dialogues, including perhaps *Protagoras, Meno, Gorgias*, and the first Book of *Republic*. In his middle period, however, when *Republic* is completed, the famous dialectical ("elenctic") method gives way to a more analytical method of the sort Aristotle will later develop so fully. In this same period, adherence to the vaunted theory of the *Forms* becomes far weaker. That it is abandoned by this time is made doubtful by the (probably) late date of the *Timaeus* where the theory is again prominent. In any case, there is no single Platonic position on the issues presumably raised by Socrates and, to this extent, the dialogues are not entirely reliable guides to "the Socratic context."

But a context is more than a set of books and will always elude merely textual modes of discovery. The circle that formed around Socrates, in an Athens that had been vanquished in the Peloponnesian Wars, included friends, not paying students; men, both young and not so young, who, if they were not "lovers of wisdom," loved that now famous gadfly who taught them what they should be. It may be assumed that young Plato was a wide-eyed and modest witness within this circle, attentive to the memories of a Socrates who had known a better age; a Socrates whose nostalgia might be fashioned into a guide for the perplexed.

In his own twenties, Socrates lived in the Athens of Pericles (490–429 B.C.) with its democratic ideals, its artistic genius, its court of the best and the brightest. Anaxagoras was not only Pericles' friend and counsellor, but the voice of a nearly official Philosophy of Reason, so much so as to enjoy the sobriquet, *nous*. Here was a time before the wars with Sparta and after the victories at Salamis and Marathon. Athens had risen to the political summit of the ancient world and was now the model culture. This was Hellenism in full flower.

But the dark clouds had already begun to form as ancient hatreds again found opportunities for expression. The Athens of Pericles had an imperial character and a cultural mission, both very costly to support. There was greed at home and envy at the borders. A plague in the city was blamed on Pericles and a petition to *ostracize* him was considered.[4] He brought matters to the point where war with Sparta could not be avoided, but he died before this very long war had completed its third year.

The observant Socrates, whose teacher by his own words was the city itself, was able to witness firsthand the historical enactment of philosophies in conflict; the collision between the confident rationalism of Anaxagoras and that sceptical theory of the fluxes made famous by Heraclitus; the collision between the moral lessons bequeathed by Homeric myths and the shrugging agnosticism of the great Sophist, Protagoras. Consider the opening and the only surviving lines of Protagoras's *On Gods:* "About the gods I cannot say either that they are or that they are not, nor how they are constituted in shape; for there is much which prevents knowledge, the unclarity of the subject and the shortness of human life."

The challenge of Sophist teaching was nothing less than the definition of Philosophy itself. Is it no more than a congeries of rhetorical devices capable of disarming the uninitiated? Is the philosopher left with the dubious distinction of knowing no more than that he knows nothing, the wisdom bestowed on the Socrates of the *Symposium?*

Athens at her peak was the very emblem of *nous*, the badge of reason itself. Athens in decline was a cauldron of intrigue and villainy, her values subjectivized beyond recognition, her aspirations confined to brute survival and the pleasures of the moment. The Socrates preserved in Plato's early dialogues has given up on the world of mere mortals and now looks for the divine within them. If life must be lived on earth, its soul trapped in the *desmoterion,* then its rule must be the rule of law, the rule of sweet reason, whose Golden String is the only one man-as-puppet can pull on and thus resist even the gods![5]

Socrates' philosophy teaches men how to live so that they will know how to die. There is no paradox here, for the whole point of life turns out to be the soul's readiness for its own liberation, its

4. The term *ostracism* refers to a ten-year sentence of exile. The political and economic climate surrounding Pericles at the time was capable of supporting any number of charges against him. The expenditures for the redesign of the Acropolis occasioned still other attacks. On these and related matters, consult the chapter on Pericles in Plutarch's *The Lives of the Noble Grecians and Romans.*

5. Plato, *Laws*, 1, 641.

own next incarnation. But a preparation of this sort cannot occur amidst moral flotsam or be left to the well-known penchants of the Plain Man. The Good Man, like the Good State, is a republic of virtue in which actions are answerable to principles. To violate these is to bring shame upon oneself. It is to corrupt what is divine within oneself and thus to incur, in Homeric fashion, the ire of the gods. True, the gods at this point form something of a convenient fiction, but behind the fiction there is for Socrates that most stark of realities in which each soul must find its way. It was Socrates who was amused to notice how the gods typically look like the residents of their patron cities.[6] The charge of heresy brought against him by thugs and villains was, in the end, ironically valid. Socrates was religious, even reverential, but his divinities were not of this world. They were in that realm of *Forms* presided over by principles that are to the mind as mathematics, and to the spirit as music.

Socrates' attitudes, then, "to experience, to man and the world," at least as these attitudes are faithfully conveyed by Plato, are more intuitive than analytical, more religious than, alas, philosophical. In his *Epistles*, some of doubtful authenticity, Plato would have readers believe that the dialogues are accurate transcriptions provided by a mere amanuensis. This is modesty bordering on self-libel, of course, but there is no reason to adopt a position at the other extreme; viz., that Socrates is little more than a *dramatis persona* giving an endearing voice to Plato's own original views. Socrates engaged in spirited dialogues, some of them certainly recovered in the *Dialogues*. It is sufficient to acknowledge in this regard that Plato's genius is manifest in his ability to express Socrates's essential insights in a manner admitting of philosophical assessment; in his ability to give them that systematic character that allows instruction in virtue even when the living example is no longer present. The *Second Epistle* must not be taken as

---

6. There is a contrapuntal relationship between heresy and reverence in the dialogues. Socrates and other participants are openly dismissive of much of the folk-religion of their countrymen, but are deeply religious in their own theology. But the matter of religious belief in ancient Greece is complex and elusive. An exceptionally coherent and documented study is Walter Burkert's *Greek Religion*, published in German in 1977 and in English in 1985. An especially instructive account is given of the crisis created by the atheistic implications of Sophist teachings (pp. 311–317). For an analysis of Plato's *Sophist*, consult Stanley Rosen's book of the same name (New Haven: Yale University Press, 1983). And lest any depiction of Sophist teaching be taken as dispository, Professor Rosen's caveat is in order: "Thus far, the attempt to pin down the sophist within a single family has been a comedy" (p. 143).

17

entirely truthful, even if authentic, where Plato is found saying that, "there is not and never will be a work of Plato; the works which now go by that name belong to Socrates, embellished and rejuvenated."[7]

But if "embellished and rejuvinated" are taken as euphemisms for "made clear and timely", then the letter leads to an important recognition; to wit, that Plato's philosophy is intended for this world too. As Burnet says of Plato's teaching,

> No one has insisted more strongly than he has on the primacy of the Theoretic Life. . . . But . . . an equal stress is laid on the duty of philosophers to descend into the Cave in turn and to rescue as many of their former fellow-prisoners as may be, even against their will. . . . [T]here was nothing at all impracticable in what Plato undertook.[8]

Still, in their attitudes toward experience, toward man, and toward the world, Socrates and Plato are in the end disciples of the same school, and Aristotle is not. A sketch of the Socratic position, as "embellished and rejuvinated" by his famous disciple, prepares the way for an understanding of Aristotle's points of departure.

It was Protagoras' famous maxim that declared man to be the measure of all things.[9] And it is Heraclitus whose "cosmic fragments" teach that no one can descend twice into the same stream.[10] The one aphorism renders epistemology a mere branch of introspective psychology, and the other gives this psychology a buzzing instability for its subject. What both have in common is the tacit acceptance of perception as both the source and the standard of the

7. Plato, *Epistles*, translated by Glenn Morrow (Indianapolis: Bobbs-Merrill, 1962). The authenticity of authorship surrounds some of the *Epistles*, but not the authenticity of the sentiments expressed. If Plato did write such modest lines—or if he wrote some other passages that would lead others to attribute this admission to him—the explanation probably can be found in his sensed debt to his teacher. Scholarship has been able to tease out at least some of the Socrates and some of the Plato in the dialogues, so that two identifies can be discerned. As noted in the chapter, much of Plato's writing took place quite some time after the death of Socrates and is, therefore, not to be regarded as a transcription recorded by an amanuensis. Even the earliest dialogues reconstruct and formalize discussions that were probably far less tidy and conclusory at the time they took place.

8. J. Burnet "Philosophy," pp. 83–84.

9. *Theaetetus*, 152.

10. Assessing the Socratic debt to the pre-Socratics is ever the more difficult in light of the skimpy remains of what was certainly an epoch of philosophical originality. About 140 fragments attributable to Heraclitus survive and can be found in *Heraclitus: The Cosmic Fragments*.

knowable. Recognized in this light, Protagoras can be seen as advancing an early form of the so-called *incorrigibility* thesis, according to which each percipient enjoys unimpeachable epistemic authority as regards his own experiences. What Smith says about his pains, pleasures, sensations is just the last word.[11] He cannot be *provably* mistaken when he claims, for example, to be in pain, for the very reality or existence or ontology of pain is necessarily conditional on its being *someone's* pain. If Protagoras' maxim is restated as, "Each perception is the ultimate measure of itself," it is true and by no means trivial. The same may be said of a version of the sort, "Man is the measure of all perceived things." But in its received form, the contention that each person has a protected proprietorship of, as it were, "his own truths"—these being the gift of experience—Protagoras' teaching could only elicit Socrates' rejection of the whole world of experience; a world, as he says in the *Theaetetus* (161), in which it would be apt to make "the dog-faced baboon" the measure of all things.[12]

Socrates, contra Heraclitus, insisted on the distinction between the mere and unconnected facts of perception, and the coherent understandings that fall within the province of mind. The distinction is pursued relentlessly in the *Theaetetus* (a dialogue of Plato's "third period", presumably), where both Protagoras and Heraclitus are subjected to scathing critiques. Socrates serves as the devil's advocate in both cases, but then exposes the errors and follies infecting even the fairest renderings of Protagoras' subjectivism and Heraclitus' theory of the fluxes. Their fatal mistake, in Socrates' account, are the adoption of sense-based theories of reality, and their failure to recognize that *perceived* reality is a world of illusion, half-truth, and self-deception. It is the world of the Plain Man, the world the philosopher must expose for the counterfeit that it is. Like Thales, who allegedly fell into a well while staring at the heavens, every true philosopher will be the subject of ridicule and will prove to be useless to those trapped in the affairs and experiences of the moment. But even those who despise and scoff at philosophers, "when they begin to reason in private about their

11. "Incorrigibility" as used here is discussed in chapter 2 of D. N. Robinson, *Philosophy of Psychology*. See also Kurt Beier's "Smart on Sensations," in C.V. Borst, ed., *The Mind/Brain Identity Theory*.
12. Socrates does not deny incorrigibility. Rather, he takes it to be just one more piece of evidence *against* sensationistic approaches to knowledge. It is just because each person does, indeed, have unique epistemological authority in the matter of his own sensations that these cannot count for *truth*.

dislike of philosophy, if they have the courage to hear the argument out, and do not run away, they grow at last strangely discontented with themselves." (*Theaetetus*, 177)[13] The world of appearances finally does not satisfy those who have even the most fleeting glimpse of a more authentic realm, the realm of truth. But this is a realm inaccessible to the senses, for it is a realm of permanence, the soul's proper setting.

The Socratic-Platonic attitude toward man and the world is grounded in and, in turn, reinforces this attitude toward experience. For all the nativistic talk about men of brass, men of gold, etc. (*Republic* III, 415),[14] the dialogues regard the human character as protean and ever in need of discipline and the purifications of philosophy. As the Stranger says in the *Sophist*, the master of the eristic art—even if he is less than a true philosopher—is a "purifier of the soul" and knows that his patient "must be purged of his prejudices" (*Sophist*, 230).[15] The prejudices themselves are deformities of the soul, self-imposed through a reliance on appearances and an uncritical acceptance of the things of the world. Again, in the *Laws*, the point is made still another way, when the Athenian stranger declares the greatest of all plagues that might befall the state to be "not faction, but rather distraction" (*Laws*, V, 744).

But the Socratic-Platonic psychology is a mixture of faction and distraction, taking the sensual and the rational sides of human nature as locked in struggle, a struggle that is, one might say, utterly non-Freudian! If the fundamental tension in psychoanalytic theory is between the Pleasure Principle and the Reality Principle, in the dialogues it is between *both* of these on the one hand, and

13. The "wisdom" imparted by philosophy would be featured in most of Aristophanes' comedies and, as was intended, would make its devotees seem like clowns. The innocent fun would help to produce a far from innocent outcome at Socrates' trial, however.

14. This heavily nativistic metaphor is declared to be a fiction within the dialogue itself. Here and elsewhere Socrates shows himself to be only a moderate on the subject of eugenic engineering. If nurturance by philosophy is to hold any promise of success, there must be good qualities to work on in the first instance. But pedigree *per se* is not a guarantee. Socrates' unbridled nativism is found in his theory of knowledge as the *reminiscence* of truths eternally possessed by souls. It is important to distinguish between "innate ideas" as knowledge inhering in soul, and some sort of biogenetic psychology grounded in pedigree. Socrates (playfully?) speaks of breeding Guardians as Glaucon has bred hunting dogs, but when the regimen facing prospective Guardians is considered, it is clear that the emphasis is to be on the *formation*, not on the "inheritance," of character.

15. Here again is the love-hate relationship with Sophists and their teachings. Greek philosophy owed much to the Sophists, even if by the time of the Academy they had become paid specialists whose only mission was to turn out well-off gentlemen skilled in scoring debater's points.

virtue on the other. The Freudian "reality" principle is scarcely a principle. It is rather a species of prudence which encourages the actor to come to terms with the expectations of his surroundings and to do nothing that will invite the rebukes and rejections of his fellows. But the summons of virtue is quite different, essentially Homeric. It places the needs of the soul above those of the body. To have the full benefits of the senses but to live without virtue is the greatest of evils, for it curses an immortal soul (*Laws* II, 661).

If virtue is the goal of any life that is to be lived as a truly human life, what then is virtue? The dialogues discuss no question at greater length and arrive at somewhat different but, on the whole, consistent answers. There is an early enumeration of the virtues in the *Protagoras* (349): wisdom, temperance, justice, courage, and holiness. The last of these is dropped later (e.g., *Republic* IV, 428), though it is implicit in the other four, and wisdom is typically asserted to be at the foundation of them all. The wisdom in question is the *phronesis* of the lawgiver (the *wise man*) or the reflective and self-critical intelligence *(sophia)* of the philosopher. It is not the factual intelligence *(episteme)* of, for example, the scientist or craftsman. Wisdom pulls together into harmony the other virtues, the other powers of the soul and imbues it with beauty. This is all movingly expressed by Socrates himself in the prayer he offers up at the conclusion of the *Phaedrus:* "Beloved Pan, and all ye other gods who haunt this place, give me beauty in the inward soul; and may the outward and inward man be at one. May I reckon the wise to be the wealthy"(279).

It is the soul that is the repository of such universal truths as might be known. Body *per se* can have no commerce with such truths, for body is only a congeries of material parts, each and all of them in a state of (Heraclitean) flux and destined to die and disappear. Socrates is never so emphatic in his Mind/Body dualism as in the *Phaedo*, where the soul is not only treated as imperishable but as recurrently incarnated in different prisons. Philosophical wisdom—the proper aim of the soul—is the wisdom of unchanging universals, and only the unity and immateriality of the soul can be conversant with knowledge of this sort. In death there is liberation, for the soul now can commune directly with its proper subjects. All faction has ended with death and the soul, "draws after her no bodily taint, having never voluntarily during life had connection with the body, which she is ever avoiding" (*Phaedo* 80).

It is at this point, too, that Socrates gives the soul over to the

21

contemplation of pure abstractions, making her the disciple of true philosophy and, to this extent, regarding the soul as having been "always engaged in the practice of dying." The subject of philosophy is just what remains when all merely earthly concerns are set aside, when both the pleasures of the body and the "reality" of time and place have been dissolved away and naught remains but a contemplation of the eternal and sublime. The departed soul enters the world of invisibles, the world of "the divine and immortal and rational ... released from the error and folly of men" (*Phaedo*, 81).

If this attitude toward human earthly life had been expressed by one of the early Fathers of the Church—and it was, indeed, expressed by most of them—it could be understood as proceeding from a certain interpretation of scripture in which the Son of God has proclaimed that his kingdom is not of this world. The context —an empire at once effete and imperiled, traditional values scorned, the foreseeable future despised—would make more intelligible this sort of resignation from life. But the Socrates of the dialogues, as well as the Socrates portrayed by Xenophon, is in fact a happy man of the world, eager to put his mark on it. He has taken important political stands in his life [16] and has shown himself to be interested and involved in the affairs of his city and his time. These two sides of the man are easily reconciled when his attitude toward the world itself is examined, an attitude that takes the world to be at once a proving ground and a classroom, a theater and a court. It would be correct to say that Socrates examines three worlds in the dialogues; the inner world of the soul wherein one's character is formed, the outer world of the state, whose proper business is the formation of character within its citizens, and that ultimate world of spirit, which earthly life must take as its goal and example if there is to be redemption. The Cosmos is ruled by rational principles, and so, too, must be the state; and so, too, must be each citizen within the state. As best as can be discerned by imperfect earthly powers, the ultimate cosmic principles are of a mathematical form and express perfected order, perfected *harmonia*. The political version or metaphor of this in the sublunary realm is justice; and, in the realm of the individual soul, *virtue*. Wisdom is at the foundation of all three. Moreover, the greatest obstacle to an understanding of all three is *appearance*. Even Glaucon recognizes that

16. Such as, for example, his opposition to the will of the Thirty Tyrants (*Apology* 32).

"the highest reach of injustice is, to be deemed just when you are not" (*Republic* II, 361), and this from a man who has still not heard a convincing argument for the superiority of a life of virtue over that of self-indulgence.

It is in Book II of *Republic* that Socrates offers his sternest rebuke of the poets and shows his impatience even, and especially, with beloved Homer.[17] The Homeric and Hesiodic accounts of the gods are condemned as grave distortions which can only corrupt the character of the young by suggesting that villainy and deception and vanity are god-like qualities. Thus, "although we are admirers of Homer, we do not admire the lying dream which Zeus sends to Agamemnon" (383) since, "God is not the author of all things, but of good only" (380).

The religion that Socrates' state would teach is metaphysical where Homer's was allegorical. The Socratic gods are remote and incorporeal, where Homer's can be found around every corner, often impelled by less than lofty motives. The Homeric world is populated by entirely human heroes, quick-tempered, lusting after honor, easily offended, demanding of tribute and booty. The Socratic world yearns for the heroic but detests the all too human. It is a world, therefore, whose guardians hold no property, whose leaders arise from a eugenically refined class, and whose social organization is communal. It is, of course, an unreal world, and Socrates admits as much: "Would a painter be any the worse because, after having delineated with consummate art an ideal of a perfectly beautiful man, he was unable to show that any such man could ever have existed?" (*Republic* v, 472).

But it is that world of perfect justice and harmony that must be the earthly goal of those whose afterlife is of paramount concern. A Spartan regimen must be instituted early in the life of a child and maintained throughout the stages of development. Musical harmonies and martial strains are to be the acoustic emblems of order and courage, the sensual dithyrambs being outlawed. Useful deceptions are not to be shunned, for, as it is permissible to lie to an enemy in order to secure victory, so also is it permissible to deceive those enemies within the human frame that compete with and stifle the virtues. A noble life is one devoted to noble things, and these are not the things of the world or the things of the senses. The

17. The target is not Homer but literalists who take the epics to be true depictions of the gods. Homer is cited more than a hundred times and in nearly all of the dialogues. In *Ion* (530), he is the most divine of the poets.

soul's proper business is to make contact with its own precious possessions, the universal and unchanging truths that abound beyond the *desmoterion*.

This is all quite Homeric, of course, once the broadsides against the poets are discounted. The entities that do the work of "soul" in the epics—*psyche, menos, lyssa, thýmos*—are constantly jumping in and out of bodies. In the Platonic account, there is a more orderly and parsimonious arrangement than in Homer's. Plato provides a tripartite division for the human soul; the rational element, designated as *logos*, and the nonrational elements of *thumos* and *epithumia*. The former in Plato retains the Homeric character of impulsive and even lustful desire, but the latter is closer to one's "heart's desire" or something willed with great feeling. These distinctive aspects of *psyche* are examined with philosophical rigor in the dialogues, but their Homeric spiritedness is retained. Death does not so much put an end to them as it frees or unharnesses them from the burdens of the flesh. On this central principle, the line extending from Homer to the *Academy* is unbroken. As P. A. Vander Waerdt has observed,

> Throughout the long tradition of Greek anthropological speculation the principles of both popular and philosophical psychology were based, virtually without exception, upon the dichotomy between rational and irrational forces in the human soul. (p. 373)[18]

Read under a certain light, the *Iliad* and *Odyssey* are emblem books in which virtue and vice are allegorized and the wages of sin assessed. All of the principals are seeking justice in these stories. All of the indignation is righteous, and if the gods are not perfect, neither are they ultimate. The Homeric and Hesiodic theogonies are blurry at the points of origin and wonderfully delphic in the catalogues of the real versus the apparent powers of the Olympians. Homer's epics are not a story told but a story unfolding, the current version ending with Odysseus home again with Penelope, his enemies vanquished. Where does the saga end? Perhaps in that world of greater justice and goodness envisaged by Socrates where

18. For a thorough discussion of the Homeric position on the fate, near and far, of *menos, lyssa, thumos*, and the rest, following the death of the body, consult chapter 3 of Bremmer's *The Early Greek Concept of the Soul*. An excellent discussion of the Platonic soul-division and its fate at the hands of later peripatetic interpreters is P. A. Vander Waerdt, "Peripatetic Soul-Division, Posidonius, and Middle Platonic Moral Psychology."

the most truthful man is most valorous, where wisdom is riches, where justice is supreme, and where philosphers are kings.

In Book v of the *Republic*, Socrates is found teaching moderation even toward one's enemies, being especially lenient toward fellow Hellenes. They should be guided by the realization that today's enemy may well be tomorrow's comrade and that, in any case, the truly innocent greatly outnumber the guilty in any war. How redolent this is of the closing lines of the *Odyssey*. Odysseus with his brave sons has nearly routed his enemies and is now closing for the kill. But Athene cries out, urging restraint. Still, Odysseus begins his descent on his foes "like a high-flown eagle," but is stopped in his tracks by a thunderbolt sent by Zeus of the wide brows, son of Kronos. Athene admonishes Odysseus once more lest Zeus be further offended.

> So spoke Athene, and with happy heart he obeyed her. And pledges for the days to come, sworn by both sides, were settled by Pallas Athene, daughter of Zeus of the aegis, who had likened herself in appearance and voice to Mentor. (*Odyssey* 545)

How distant all of this seems from the concerns that occupied Aristotle, at least as these are conveyed by his extant works. The distance will be gauged again in chapter 4. But from what is found in these works, from comments provided by near and more remote ancient writers, and from what can safely be conjectured about Aristotle's now missing treatises, it is clear that the distance was once not so great. As Sir David Ross observed, Aristotle's intellectual development moved "from otherworldliness towards an intense interest in the concrete facts,"[19] but the Aristotle of the *Protrepticus*, as will be noted in later chapters, retains the ultimate commitment of his teacher and his teacher's teacher.

Just where is he to be located within the larger ancient Greek and Socratic contexts briefly examined in this and the preceding chapters? Marjorie Grene's thesis—that what were problems for Plato and Socrates just aren't Aristotle's problems[20]—is inviting, but seems finally to be sound only at a level of analysis that is, itself, less than compelling. What were problems, after all, for Socrates and Plato remain central to the program of philosophy: the problem of knowledge (maturing into epistemology), the prob-

19. Sir David Ross, *Aristotle*. The edition used here is the paperback edition. The quotation is taken from p. 19.
20. Grene, *Portrait of Aristotle*, p. 41.

lem of conduct (ethics), the problem of governance (political science).[21] These are, needless to say, central to Aristotle's program as well, even if Aristotle's approach turns out to be radically different. Yet, in this radical difference in approach, there is a measure of the movement not only away from the teachings of the Academy but from what was finally the ancient Greek perspective at large. The movement is away from the authority of tradition, away from the conviction that ignorance will be vanquished by the Heroes of Wisdom the way Troy was defeated by the Heroes of Homer.

There is no Wise Man to rely on in Aristotle's major works, nor is there confidence in the power of talk—dialectical or otherwise—to settle matters of fact.[22] There is, moreover, a respect bordering on passion for the world of sense, the world of nature. There is a realism and earthiness. Mathematical abstractions are no longer the first and final standards of knowledge. The arts of knowing have been transformed into sciences, these classified by various mental faculties whose principles of operation become the subject of still other disciplines.

How are these developments to be understood? There is first, of course, Aristotle's own genius which could never content itself with orthodox discipleship. Ingemar Düring was persuaded that this genius surfaced early enough to have influenced the course of Plato's later dialogues.[23] The enduring influence of Werner Jaeger's *Aristotle*,[24] though not without its problems and its critics,[25] has made the received Aristotle the product of a continuing intellectual development; first the loyal student of the Academy whose own "esoteric" or popular works (now lost but for some fragments) are Platonic in texture and in temper. Next there is the Aristotle of the years away from Athens, in Assos and Lesbos, steeped in naturalistic studies. Finally, there is the Aristotle who is master of his own school in Athens, favored by Alexander the Great, and systematiz-

21. This division is discussed and developed in chapters 2 and 3 of my *An Intellectual History of Psychology*.
22. Evidence that Aristotle composed dialogues early in his career is circumstantial and, in the absence of textual evidence, there is no reason to assume that such dialogues would have been more than exercises. Refer also to note 26 below for Anton-Hermann Chroust's comment on this same matter.
23. Ingemar Düring, "Aristotle and Plato in the Mid-Fourth Century", pp. 109–120.
24. Werner Jaeger, *Aristotle: Fundamentals of the History of His Development*. This is the "classic" biography, the one other biographers have been correcting, supporting, and interpreting for half a century.
25. Grene *(Portrait of Aristotle)* summarizes the major evidence favoring and opposing Professor Jaeger's "genetic" thesis.

ing philosophy, science, political theory, and ethics as a seasoned polymath with his own independent identity.

Whether or not this "genetic" account is correct in detail or even in general, the *corpus* of Aristotle's works is unmistakably beholden to Plato's teaching for much of its subject matter, for some of its conclusions, and for most of its critical originality. But this all has to do with pieces and parts, and not with what is *Aristotelian* in Aristotle's works. Professor Jaeger's interesting discovery of Aristotle's use of "we" early in the *Metaphysics* and "they" later, when discussing Platonist teaching, may indeed support a genetic theory, but both the early and the late parts of the *Metaphysics* are "Aristotelian" in a manner that none of the dialogues is. The point here, perhaps too obvious to warrant repetition, is that the "Platonic Aristotle" is as clearly Aristotle as is Aristotle the scientist, the psychologist, the logician.

His father, Nichomachus, was a successful physician, well enough known to serve as court physician to Amyntas III of Macedonia, father of Philip and grandfather of Alexander. It is not clear that Nichomachus' profession was the source of Aristotle's lifelong interest in the biological sciences, though some influence of this sort is doubtless. How he found his way to the Academy in 367 B.C. remains unclear. His father may have died just before this, for it was Aristotle's brother-in-law, Proxenus, who accompanied the young pupil to Athens.[26] He is found leaving the Academy some twenty years later (348–47 B.C.), returning to found the Lyceum some thirteen years after that. The triumphs of Alexander would create great enmities within Athens between pro- and anti-Macedonian factions. Aristotle was readily (if rashly) identified with the latter. Might this political climate have moved Aristotle a safe distance away from those issues which had victimized Socrates in the same city? Single-cause theories of genius never ring true. Nichomachus' profession may have had a small part to play in Aristotle's later scientific work, and the anti-Macedonian climate of Athens may have led Aristotle to delete from his work discussions that could have been all too conveniently misconstrued. But

26. This and related matters are discussed and fully documented in Anton-Hermann Chroust, *Aristotle: New Light on His Life and On Some of His Lost Works*, vol. 1. Professor Chroust offers this telling note: "The discussion of earlier philosophers, to be sure, is for Aristotle still a dialectical debate—in this sense he is always Plato's disciple—but this debate is merely preliminary to the 'prosaic work' of philosophy and hence no longer the whole or even the main issue" (p. 411).

with such contextual factors noted, it is the independence of his genius that asserts itself in his major works. His is not a philosophy designed to teach one how to die; less is it a nostalgic search through the epics for worthy types who may never have lived. With Aristotle, the mathematical and allegorical phases of philosophical self-examination give way to a naturalistic and progressive program of research. The model of truth is no longer to be searched for in ethereal abstractions; it is to be found in the knowable Cosmos, in the kingdoms of life, in the processes of growth and decay and renewal, in the operations of the knowing mind. Through these, it becomes possible to discover the great principle that stands behind them and gives order and meaning to the rest. Aristotle, who longed as deeply as Plato to discover this principle, would find it at work no less in the cuttlefish off the shores of the Aegaean than in the rational powers of the human mind.

THREE

Aristotle's Modes of Inquiry and Explanation

One of the earliest authoritative listings of Aristotle's works was provided by Diogenes Laertius in the third century A.D., and there is good reason to consider it incomplete.[1] The record available in the penultimate decade of the twentieth century is even less complete. But on the major scientific, ethical, political, and psychological questions, the surviving works of Aristotle are sufficiently consistent as to leave little doubt about his mature positions. Equally doubtless is his commitment to reconstruct philosophy and education along lines different from those drawn by his own teachers. This is evident in his writings on logic—his *Organon*—which attempt to establish the methodological canons appropriate to the

---

1. The chronology of Aristotle's writings remains a subject of scholarly interest. Sir David Ross' *Aristotle* (pp. 7–19) provides an accessible and only slightly dated summary of the matter. The translation of Diogenes Laertius' *Lives of Eminent Philosophers* used here is R. D. Hicks, for the Loeb Classical Library. Aristotle is covered in book 5, vol. 1. Diogenes Laertius cites more than 156 works by Aristotle, most of them containing more than one book and the total yielding 445,270 lines (p. 475). The same author concludes that nearly 400 writings ("counting those only the genuineness of which is not disputed," p. 481) are attributable to Aristotle. What is clear from all this is that establishing even a flawless chronology of the surviving works would still leave unsettled the question of the various positions and the arguments developed by Aristotle in the many now lost works.

29

major fields of inquiry.[2] The purely formal logic of the syllogism is developed primarily in his *Prior Analytics*. It is, however, in his *Posterior Analytics* that he constructs a philosophy of explanation that is carried over into his major works on science, ethics, and psychology. In the background of this treatise are all the conundrums that the Socratics found to be so daunting, but Aristotle will not be sidetracked by them as he presses on toward what is finally a practical, commonsense approach, though one that is rigorously systematic. The treatise itself opens on just such a note: "All teaching and all intellectual learning come about from already existing knowledge" (71ᵃ 1).

Knowledge has a starting point that must be granted, and thus a complete scepticism is simply rejected as self-refuting. Nonetheless, it is also the case that there are different *senses* of knowing, and so it is entirely possible—and even quite common—for someone to know something in one sense and not know it in another. Accordingly, the vexing problem of Plato's *Meno* is seen to arise from a conflation of the different sense of knowing (*Post. Anal.* 71ᵃ 25–30).[3] It is interesting that, at the place in *Meno* where the challenge is laid down, Socrates launches into a story told about the immortal soul by priests and priestesses—this before he begins his famous interrogation of Meno's servant-boy. Aristotle, however, finds his own solutions closer to his earthly home! Thus, one who knows by prior instruction that the angles of a triangle contain 180 degrees, knows that this is so for *this* triangle. Although one could, by measurement, come to know that this is so for a given triangle, without the benefit of mathematical demonstration one would not know it is so for any other triangle. Clearly, if Smith and Jones both know that the angles of triangle A add to 180 degrees, then they both know it. But if Smith knows it as a consequence of measuring the angles of triangle A, whereas Jones knows it of triangle A as a deduction from a universal premise, then what Smith and Jones know of triangle A is known in *different senses*.

The species of knowledge examined in the *Posterior Analytics*

2. The logical treatises include *Categories, On Interpretation, Prior Analytics, Posterior Analytics, Topics,* and *Sophistical Refutations*. All translations referred to here and in other chapters of the book are taken from the two-volume *The Complete Works of Aristotle*, edited by Jonathan Barnes.

3. Meno's taunt is to the effect that, if Socrates knows what he is looking for, there is no reason to undertake a search, but, if he does not know what he is looking for, there is simply no basis upon which to begin the search (*Meno*, 80–81; Jowett translation in *The Dialogues of Plato*).

Aristotle refers to as *demonstration,* and it is this that leads to *understanding.* Thus, understanding is knowing something in a specific way; viz., through demonstration. To understand is to be aware of this: that the "because of which the object is," just *is* its explanation, and that "it is not possible for this to be otherwise" than it is. (*Post. Anal.* 70^b 10–15) The requirement that understanding *simpliciter* carries with it the knowledge that what is could not be otherwise, arises from another feature of Aristotle's theory. To understand something—any particular thing or event—is to recognize it as an instance of a universal class or (scientifically) an instantiation of a universal law. The form of (demonstrative) explanations is syllogistic. The major premise in this case is a universal law or universalized proposition. The thing or event to be explained is then inserted as the factual content of the minor premise. If it is true, and if the universal proposition or law inserted as the major premise is also true, then the demonstration succeeds.[4] But if the universal law is true, then the event or thing in question could not, in fact, be otherwise.

Aristotle is careful to spell out the essential components of demonstrative understanding (*Post. Anal.* 70^b 10–72^a 30). Such understanding must be based upon what is true, what is "primitive," what is "familiar" and "prior to," and what is "explanatory". That understanding must be based upon what is true, is obvious. By "primitive," Aristotle refers to certain nondemonstrable assumptions without which any and every attempt at understanding would become lost in a sea of infinite regressions. As noted, knowledge must have a starting point, and each case has its own "primitives" as starting points.

The primitives are *principles* which, in demonstrative modes of understanding, take the form of *propositions.* These propositions are "immediate" in that no other proposition is required as a condition of beginning the demonstration. Aristotle uses the term *posit* to stand for those immediate propositions (now immediate deductive principles) that are not themselves provable but that also need not be fully understood by those who would understand the demonstration; e.g., the mathematician's assertion that a "unit" is that which cannot be divided. Some deductive principles, how-

---

4. In this, Aristotle lays the foundations for that "nomological-deductive" model of scientific explanation that has been so influential in philosophy of science. It is most fully developed in modern times by Carl Hempel. See, for example, his *Aspects of Scientific Explanation and Other Essays in the Philosophy of Science.*

ever, must be understood if the demonstration is to be comprehended, and these are what Aristotle calls *axioms*.

There are posits that are assertoric in that they claim that something either is or is not the case, and these qualify as *suppositions*.
Others are not, and serve as primitive *definitions*. To say, then, as
Aristotle does, that understanding depends on what is "primitive"
is to build into all demonstrative understanding a fixed logical
structure that is axiomatic, *a priori*, syllogistic. In saying that understanding depends also on what is "prior and familiar," Aristotle
makes the distinction between familiarity *simpliciter* and familiarity in the relative sense. In the latter case, things are more familiar
when they are directly perceptible; e.g., *that* chair. But they are
prior and more familiar *simpliciter* when they are universals; e.g.,
chair. An understanding of chairs, for example, proceeds on the
(truthful) assumption that particular (perceptible) things answering to the definition of the universal class, "chair," are covered by
immutable principles. When understood in these terms and in terms
of the "because of which," chairs are *demonstratively* understood.

Aristotle recognized the apparent circularity here and the criti-
cisms likely to arise from Megaric and Sophist quarters. The critic's gambit is straightforward:

1. According to Aristotle, demonstrative understanding involves
principles.

2. Principles include "primitives" that are not themselves demonstrable.

3. If there are no primitives, then nothing posterior can be
understood, for such a thing will have no principles to explain it.

4. If there are primitives, these, too, are posterior to their own
prior (but unknowable) primitives.

5. Thus, the analysis either calls for an infinite regress or for
perpetual ignorance.

The defect in this criticism, according to Aristotle, is that the
critic assumes that all understanding is demonstrative—which, if
true, would indeed yield the infinite regression. However, Aristotle
argues that all understanding is *not* demonstrative, that the "immediates" are nondemonstrable, and that demonstrative arguments "come to a stop" at a certain point (*Post. Anal.* 72^b 20–25).

This, to be sure, is not a theory of innate ideas or a veiled advocacy of Platonic "Forms" residing within the soul prior to all experience. Again, the "immediates" are *principles* (posits) that function within demonstrative explanations as suppositions or definitions or originating axioms. The very search for a demonstrative explanation requires all of this and it is here that the analysis of necessary principles or posits "comes to a stop."[5]

Part of the distinction between demonstrative and nondemonstrative modes of understanding is grounded in the difference between universals and "accidentals." Aristotle defines the universal as that which not only belongs to something in every case but belongs "in itself and as such" (*Post. Anal.* 73[b] 25). It is not merely (contingently) the case that straightness and curvedness happen to be reliably associated with lines. Rather, these are aspects of lines *as such* and stand, therefore, as *necessary* attributes. They are part of the very definition of *line*, and are not mere correlates or "accidentals." Of course, it may happen by chance that something is true of some object and, on the basis of this, unfailing deductions might follow. A given isosceles triangle may have two angles that add to 90 degrees or 60 degrees. But such specific attributes are not necessary parts of the definition of isosceles triangles generically and do not, therefore, enter into a demonstrative understanding of such triangles. Only when the attributes are what they are *primitively* do they enter into demonstrative understanding. And attributes that are what they are *primitively* could not be otherwise. It is in this respect that "demonstrative understanding depends on necessary principles" (*Post. Anal.* 74[b] 5). With accidentals, however, the association is not by definition or in itself or essential. Here, demonstrative modes of understanding are simply out of place. As a result of this, accidentals are not central to the mission of *scientific* inquiry, for the goal of science is demonstrative understanding.[6]

5. There is an interesting similarity between Aristotle's "immediates" and those famous principles of *common sense* developed and defended in the eighteenth century by Thomas Reid. Reid explained the principles of common sense as those one is under an obligation to take for granted in all of the affairs of life, and exemplified them in such necessary and unanalyzed presuppositions as the Law of Contradiction. The principles are not to be confused with opinions or matters of taste or, indeed, anything that can be disputed. They are akin in this regard to Locke's notion of the "original acts" of the mind, to Descartes' native concepts, and at least to some of Kant's *pure categories* of the understanding. For Reid's discussion of the principles of common sense, see Thomas Reid, *An Inquiry into the Human Mind on the Principles of Common Sense.*

6. Aristotle claims that scientific explanations are concerned with what belongs to things in themselves and as such. (*Post. Anal.* 75[a] 30–35) Events or attributes that are

It is within the *Posterior Analytics*, too, that Aristotle invokes a psychological criterion as a defense against the persistent sceptic. This is found at 76^b 10–30, where he is summarizing the three chief ingredients of every demonstrative science. There is, first, what that science posits *to be*, i.e., the basic ontology of the science. This ontological positing includes a specification of those attributes that belong to each thing in itself and not accidentally or contingently. Next, there are the *common axioms* of the demonstrative science, akin to what in Euclid's geometry are called the "common notions." An example Aristotle offers in several places is the equality that remains when equals are subtracted from equals.[7] Third, every demonstrative science takes certain attributes as signifying something about the entity whose attributes these are.

At this point, however, Aristotle departs from the essentially logical strictures he has been developing and inserts the following claim: "What necessarily is the case because of itself and necessarily seems to be the case is not a supposition or a postulate. For demonstration is not addressed to external argument—but to argument in the soul" (*Post. Anal.* 76^b 25–30).

Now, just what is this "argument in the soul"? It is nothing less than that rational faculty, that capacity for logical thought and for the comprehension of universal propositions, that must be taken for granted as a condition of even addressing the nature of demonstrative science. Again, there is no backsliding here into some species of Platonic nativism. There is, however, a full respect for the legitimacy of the problems raised in the *Meno*. If a logical demonstration is to succeed, it must succeed "in the soul," for certainties and necessities are not to be found in externals. But the soul is not born with the conclusions in question, for this would lead to the absurd conclusion that man possesses the most precise forms of knowledge but doesn't notice it! (*Post. Anal.* 99^b 25–30) Yet, it is equally absurd to assume that there is at one moment, so to speak, abject ignorance and, at the next, demonstrative understanding

---

accidental do not hold necessarily and, therefore, an explanation is really not to be had, for one does not know why the conclusion of the syllogism holds when it does. If, for example, men are *usually* mortal, the death of Socrates is inexplicable.

7. The analogy here has been treated with great care and perspicuity by Alfonso Gomez-Lobo in "Aristotle's Hypotheses and the Euclidean Postulates." Gomez-Lobo establishes that Euclid's own system was original and was not mechanically derived from Aristotle's. He also shows, however, that Aristotle's own position is consistent with the practices of the ancient Greek mathematicians whom both Aristotle and Euclid would consult.

arising from nothing more than brute sensory events. What must be the case, then, is that human beings have a cognitive *capacity* by which the (perceptual) registration of externals leads to their storage in memory, this giving rise to *experience*, and from this— "or from the whole universal that has come to rest in the soul"—a veritable principle of understanding arises (*Post. Anal.* 100 1–10).

Under one light, this sort of analysis would seem to render even the most formal modes of argument alarmingly "subjective," but this would be to misplace Aristotle's emphasis. The truth of conclusions grounded in true premises and proceeding from valid syllogisms is not solely a property or state of the mind that apprehends it, but a property of logic itself. It is, however, only by way of the rational capacities of man that such is known. One might say that the deductive science of geometry is entirely unknown among all nonhuman animals and perhaps among the majority of human beings. Nevertheless, the truths of this science are indubitable and demonstrable. The truths are no more "subjective" for being apprehended by the human mind than they are merely "probable" for not being apprehended by 100 percent of the human race.

As regards "the whole universal that has come to rest in the soul" there is room for conjecture. It was a maxim of the Aristotelians of the Scholastic age that, *Abstrahentium non est mendacium*. Although the senses can respond only to particulars, the mind is able to abstract the universal from these impressions, and the resulting concept "is no lie"; i.e., what the mind has abstracted really exists, though the universal is not accessible to mere perceptual processes. Aristotle, of course, has no patience with the notion of disembodied "true Forms," and he went so far as to extricate the good name of Socrates from the theory that asserts as much: "Socrates did not make the universals or the definitions exist apart; his successors, however, gave them separate existence, and this was the kind of thing they called Ideas."[8]

Aristotle's own position is, again, of the common sense variety. The world, as the ordinary percipient can know it and as any science might explain it, is the world that is given in experience. This is a world of individual entities, the sorts of things to which the senses are responsive. However, it is also a fact of experience that entire ensembles of things are found to share certain features and, thus, to comprise a *genus* or universal class. These commonal-

8. *Metaphysics*, Book XIII, 1078[b] 30.

ities are sorted out *in* the mind but are not manufactured or created *by* the mind. They are real, not ideal, and they are universals, though with no possible existence apart from the particulars that instantiate them. As he notes in the *Physics*, children early in life call all men "father" and all women "mother," distinguishing within this genus only later and after frequent experiences.[9]

Indeed, Aristotle's metaphysics would be a rather plain affair— not radically different from, say, Hume's—if he had limited his ontology to the material and physical contents of the world of experience. But he makes clear in many places that explanations grounded solely in the properties of matter are incomplete and deceiving. In Book I of the *Metaphysics*, for example, he reviews earlier materialistic theories of causation, such as that defended by Anaxagoras, and concludes:

> From these facts one might think that the only cause is the so-called material cause. . . . However true it may be that all generation and destruction proceed from some one or more elements, why does this happen and what is the cause? . . . [N]either the wood nor the bronze causes the change of either of them, nor does the wood manufacture a bed and the bronze a statue." (984ª 17–25)[10]

Or, as he states in the *Physics*, "If the ship-building art were in the wood, it would produce the same results by nature" (199ᵇ 28).

For Aristotle, "cause" *(aitia)* is not a univocal term but one that refers to radically different sources of movement and change. The natural sciences are suited to an examination of that aspect of what might be called the overall causal context that is merely material or physical. Were there no more to it than that, then the "First Philosophy" would be physics, and the only science would be natural science. But the world as it is actually found—including, and especially, that part of the world in which animal and human

9. *Physics* 184ᵇ 13.

10. The overall organization of Aristotle's *Metaphysics* has been examined frequently over the years in an attempt to account for the abrupt transition between successive books and the apparent nonsequentiality of their composition. Consult Joseph Owens, *The Doctrine of Being in the Aristotlelian Metaphysics*. In this important work, Father Owens convincingly defends the notion that the *Metaphysics* is essentially an organized set of school texts, each book providing the student with redactions of lectures on the "First Philosophy". The movement, then, is from critical appraisals of what earlier thinkers have taught to concluding discussions of the unmoved mover. The progression is from *phusis* to *sophia*, where the latter comprehends an awareness of the transcendent and ultimate causes of things.

forms of life produce their effects—is inexplicable merely in terms of matter in motion. Wood is a "cause" of ships and bronze of statues only in the sense of such items having to be constituted of *something*, but not in the sense of matter *qua* matter having ends or purposes. The art of shipbuilding is not in the wood but in the builder, and one simply does not begin to explain the existence of ships in the world until one searches for non-material principles of causation. The student of nature is obliged to know only those things that "do not exist apart from matter," but of that whose essence and existence are separable from matter, "it is the business of first philosophy to define" (*Physics* 194^b 10–15).

This matter will be taken up again in the next chapter, but it is important at this point to recognize a subtle distinction Aristotle seems to be making as regards the forms of explanation proper to each domain of inquiry. As he makes clear in every place where the doctrine of the four causes is discussed, an event is not fully explained unless all four causes have been identified. Physical phenomena, therefore, also require explanations that go beyond material causation. Nonetheless, the student of nature *as a student of nature only*, is not obliged to consider that which exists apart from matter or which is in principle separable from matter. Phenomena of this sort fall within the province of metaphysics (the "first philosophy").

Contrary to conventional interpretations, then, it would seem that Aristotle does not require the natural scientist *qua* natural scientist to deal with metaphysical considerations; but, at the same time, he does not expect the natural sciences qua natural sciences to be able to provide full explanations even of those phenomena that otherwise fall within their province.

Aristotle's theory of "the four causes" is not as tidy as accounts of it often make it seem.[11] At a superficial level, the material, formal, efficient, and final causes appear to be entirely different from one another and easily partitioned within the overal causal context. Aristotle encourages just such expectations when he summarizes his causal theory in Book II of the *Physics* 194^b 15–195^b 30. Thus, the cause of a silver bowl is silver, in that it is out of silver that the bowl comes to be and persists. Silver, then, is the *material* cause of the bowl. But silver can come in sheets or be worked into

11. Some of the complexities of the theory are unraveled in chapter 2 of D. N. Robinson, *Philosophy of Psychology*.

coins, etc., and not be a bowl. To qualify as "bowl," a thing must have a form of a certain kind, and so, too, with everything else. Accordingly, a thing is what it is because it satisfies certain formal criteria, these standing, then, as the *formal* cause of the thing in question. Thus, the ratio 2:1 is the *form* of the octave and an essential part of its very definition. Then, too, there are the actual hammerings and shapings of silver that finally work it into a bowl, these physical transactions constituting the *efficient* cause. It is in this sense that parents are the efficient cause of offspring. At last there is the *final* cause to consider, the "why" of the thing, the *that for the sake of which* something is done or happens or is brought about. One exercises *in order that* one will be healthy, and one works on silver and shapes and ornaments it *so that* there will be a beautiful bowl.

Once this overview is put aside in favor of a closer analysis of Aristotle's theory of causation, the partitions become more elastic and any number of qualifications must be considered. Distinctions must be made, first of all, between "proper" causes and mere correlates or accidents. One can say, for example, that Polyclitus caused the statue, or that a sculptor caused the statue, or that a human being caused the statue, or that a pale human being caused the statue. Clearly, there is no causal connection between being pale or being a human being and being causally necessary for that statue. For the given statue, the correct account is that it was caused by *Polyclitus the sculptor* (*Physics* 195^b 12).

Additionally, chance and spontaneity must be distinguished from proper causes. Aristotle speaks of the man who sets out to collect money for a scheduled feast. He goes to specific subscribers for this purpose, but he visits another person for entirely different reasons —only then to discover that he can obtain funds, here, too. If obtaining subscriptions is goal A, and if the purpose in visiting this particular person was goal B, then the unplanned success in reaching goal A must be considered as resulting from chance. What all such events have in common is an outcome not envisaged by the actor and not part of the means-ends sequence the actor has framed. Understood this way, chance is regarded as operating only where there is choice. "Thus an inanimate thing or a beast or a child cannot do anything by chance, because it is incapable of choice" (*Physics* 197^b 6).

The same is not the case, however, with *spontaneity*, which is in evidence in the animal and even in the inanimate domains. A

38

falling stone might strike a man, but not *for the sake* of this, just as a horse might run to a place of safety without having safety as an end. Only creatures with the capacity of choice ever may be said to do something "in vain," and it is these creatures that can be aided or thwarted therefore by chance. There is nothing in a chance occurrence that is contrary to the very nature of the things or events in question. The term "spontaneity," however, is applicable to what is contrary to the nature of the case or grossly at variance with what occurs naturally "for the sake of" something else.

The ends or purposes served by events fall into different categories. Some such ends are what they are by nature, as in the case of plants growing leaves to shade their fruit. Others proceed from deliberation; e.g., housebuilding. In all such instances, a certain kind of outcome is anticipated in all of the steps leading to the goal. The anticipated thing is knowable by its *form;* e.g., the silver bowl. Now, if the goal is to create an item that will hold, say, fruit, then the bowl-form is desired whether or not it is made of silver. Thus, "since nature is twofold, the matter and the form, of which the latter is the end, and since all the rest is for the sake of the end, the form must be the cause in the sense of that for the sake of which" (*Physics* 199ᵃ 30–33). Note, then, how the formal and final causes in such a case resist sharp division.

It is important to recognize also the mixed sense in which Aristotle's final causes stand as a *good* toward which the sequence of actions or events is aiming. The general principle is a Socratic one and is stated explicitly in the dialogue *Gorgias* (468; 499) where human actions are under consideration.[12] And, as Socrates does not declare that the perceived or imagined good in all cases is, in fact, good, so too does Aristotle note that, in these instances, it makes no difference whether something is called the good or the *apparent* good (*Metaphysics* 1013ᵇ 25). But a further distinction is needed here between the outcomes produced by nature and those produced by human deliberation and intention. In both cases, there is *action for an end.* It is obvious that the nearly perfect adaptation of plants and animals to their surroundings is not the result of accident or chance or spontaneity, but has arisen from processes aiming toward

12. *Gorgias,* translated by Benjamin Jowett in vol. 1, *The Dialogues of Plato.* At 468, Socrates is found telling Polus that men always act for the sake of the good—or their own perceived good—even in such instances as homicide. Socrates is not taking the position that the actor's determination of what is good in such cases is correct; only that the action proceeds from such a determination.

this end. What is good in this is what is *fitting* or what promotes the health and perpetuation of nature's creations. As in the case of human ambitions, so too in nature there can be mistakes and monstrous consequences, but these are exceptions that prove the rule.

> For those things are natural which, by a continuous movement originated from an internal principle, arrive at some end; the same end is not reached from every principle, nor any chance end, but always the tendency in each is towards the same end, if there is no impediment. (*Physics* 199^b 15–19)

The commonsense view defended by Aristotle is that the (mere) odds are entirely against fitness arising accidentally. It would be as preposterous to suggest that a tragedy by Sophocles arose from the spontaneous arrangements of words falling onto a clay surface. Natural events unfold according to principles which, when fully comprehended, are found to include a final cause. There will be the occasional exception, the occasional mistake. There may also be impediments placed in the way and these might serve as an artificial barrier to the realization of ends. But in the very great majority of cases, the outcomes of natural processes answer to a *telos* that is expressed by the very form and fitness of nature's productions.[13]

A central question arising in light of Aristotle's theory of causation is whether the relationship between cause and effect is one of necessity or merely one of contingency. Is Aristotle's position that the laws governing things just happen to be what they are or that they could not be otherwise? Stated another way, to what extent is Aristotle's position that of the "hard determinist"?

Necessity figures in Aristotle's metaphysical and logical writings in three distinct ways. There is, of course, that purely *logical* necessity that ties deductions to premises. *If* all men are mortal, and *if* Socrates is a man, then *necessarily* Socrates is mortal. No explanation of necessity is possible here beyond the very nature of rational thought itself. Then there is what Aristotle refers to as *hypothetical necessity* or "what is necessary on a hypothesis" (*Physics* 200^a 13). If a house is to be built, necessarily there must be tools and mate-

---

13. As Jonathan Barnes has written, "Aristotle does not, or need not, admit random or causeless events into his world. But he does allow that not all events are amenable to scientific understanding, for not everything exhibits the sort of regularity which science requires," in Jonathan Barnes, *Aristotle*, p. 57.

rials. If wood is to be sawed, necessarily the saw must be harder than the wood. This then leads to a third sense of "necessity" which, at one level, is simply lexical, but at another entirely natural.

The example of a saw is Aristotle's own and will be serviceable. To name an item a "saw" is to specify a function which gives meaning to the name. Thus, a saw is that which cuts through wood cleanly. There is, therefore, a species of definitional necessity that is carried along by the word itself, since a saw cuts wood *by defini-tion*. In this sense, saws cut wood necessarily in just the respect that unmarried men are bachelors, necessarily. But there is more to it than this, for the effect a saw has on wood is a matter of natural fact, and not merely a linguistic convention. Saws do cut through wood; for all practical purposes, saws *always* cut through wood. It is in the nature of the material (iron) of which a saw is made that it will cut cleanly though such softer material as wood. Thus, Aristotle concludes,

> The necessary in nature, then, is plainly what we call by the name of matter and the changes in it. . . . Perhaps the necessary is present also in the definition. . . . For in the definition too there are some parts that stand as matter. (*Physics* 200ª 32–200ᵇ 7

There are natural necessities occasioned by the nature of matter itself, and it is the mission of science to discover these and incorporate them into ever more general systems of explanation, ever more general laws. The *natural* necessities inhere in matter as such, and are not to be confused with logical abstractions or lexical conventions. Certain material properties guarantee outcomes with a reliability scarcely distinguishable from logical entailments, and this guarantee constitutes a natural necessity. At another level, the conventions of language record these reliabilities in the form of definitions. The definition of "saw" specifies functions arising out of matter (iron) of which saws are made.

How do the "final" causes fit into this scheme? Saws are made of iron, of course, *in order that* wood might be cleanly cut. And some birds have webbed feet *in order that* they might swim. In nature, as in art, the evidence of purpose is everywhere. But the temptation must be resisted which would have Aristotle personalizing these purposes. Jonathan Barnes states the matter clearly:

"Nature does nothing in vain" is a regulative principle for scientific enquiry. Aristotle knows that some aspects of nature are functionless. But he recognizes that a grasp of function is crucial to an understanding of nature. His slogans about the prudence of Nature are not pieces of childish superstition, but reminders of a central task of the natural scientist.[14]

On Aristotle's account, knowledge, or (more grandly) wisdom, falls into three categories or domains of inquiry: the theoretic, the practical, and the productive. The practical sciences are concerned with action, with bringing certain states of affairs into being. It is moral philosophy that must establish the regulative principles in this domain. The productive sciences, as the term suggests, bring actual *things* into being, from poetry and drama to the Acropolis itself. Here, too, there are principles that dictate the best forms and arrangements for the purposes that are to be served. There are, after all, not only houses but good and bad houses. It is only theoretical science, however, that has knowledge for its own sake as its end. This science certainly aids those engaged in productive and practical pursuits, but this is not why it is cultivated. It is cultivated because, "All men by nature desire to know,"[15] which means, finally, that human nature, by its very nature, necessarily seeks truth and finds its very meaning in the speculative life.

The speculative life, however, is not an inward-looking affair, aloof and hostile to the external world and to the perceptions that make it knowable. Science for Aristotle is, after all, about *something*, and that something is the universe and its contents, living and dead. The generalizations that become installed as scientific laws are generalizations from observed facts, and Aristotle shows little patience for arguments that deny the validity of such observations. The creatures of nature are endowed with sensory capacities vital to their survival, and this survival would be simply impossible were the data of perception illusory. Human perception, too, is the exercise of a faculty fitted out by nature to perform functions on which life itself depends. The evidence of perception, to serve the purposes of life, must be more than a dreamy fiction.

14. Barnes, *Aristotle*, p. 77.
15. *Metaphysics*, Book I, 1. The brief discussion (pp. 57–60) in Barnes' *Aristotle*, is illuminating on this point. But if one regards Aristotle as something of a commonsense realist, which would seem to be the position he adopts in his biological and naturalistic treatises, then his nonsceptical endorsement of observational modes of inquiry requires little by way of explanation.

The natural sciences, for Aristotle, are "theoretical" not in the sense of being abstract or ideal or impractical, but in the sense of defining the nature of the creature that pursues them. The desire to know is human *by nature* in just the way that flight is avian *by nature*. It is a primitive principle of human psychology and not reducible to some nonhuman or nonpsychological attribute. As the Greeks of the Homeric epoch invented a religion that would make them more at home in the world, Aristotle developed a scientific perspective that made the world intelligible to man and man intelligible to himself. It yields a world of knowable and orderly arrangements, governed by universal or at least nearly invariant principles that point to specific ends. Surrounding and invading this ultimate reality are any number of distracting accidents and spontaneities. The task of science is to refine the methods by which these deviations are set aside and the genuinely causal principles are clearly discerned. When they are, reality becomes explicable. The terms of explanation are the laws of science, and the form of explanation is deductive logic. The extent to which psychology can and cannot be fit into this scheme is explored in the remaining chapters.

FOUR

Psychology as a Natural Science: Ethology and Psychobiology

"Every realm of nature is marvellous . . . so we should venture on the study of every kind of animal without distaste; for each and all will reveal to us something natural and something beautiful. If any person thinks the examination of the rest of the animal kingdom an unworthy task, he must hold in like disesteem the study of man" (*Parts of Animals* 645ᵃ 17–27).

It is a mark of Aristotle's intellectual independence that, after no less than twenty years of instruction in the Academy, he would arrive at a conception of soul so radically different from the Socratic one passed down in Plato's dialogues. It is useful to return to certain points made in chapter 2 before considering Aristotle's naturalistic psychology.

When, in the opening lines of his *Metaphysics*, Aristotle observes that the delight persons take in their senses is an example of the fact that "all men by nature desire to know," his meaning must be understood at more than one level. The delight taken in experience is evidence of a *desire*, not of the validity of the knowledge thereby received. The claim, therefore, is not grounded in a radical empiricism. Rather, it is part of the very definition of man; more generally, of the animal kingdom itself. Desiring to know and taking pleasure in sensory experience are *dispositions,* and mark out the very *character* of the class, *all men.* The sensual aspect is more widely shared and marks out the very character of the class *animal.* As he says in *On the Soul,* "it is the possession of sensation that leads us for the first time to speak of living things as *animals"* (413 [b] 1). He makes the same point in his *Sense and Sensibilia:* "Sensation must, indeed, be attributed to all animals as such, for by its presence or absence we distinguish between what is and what is not animal" (436 [b] 10).[1]

The perspective here is that of the biologist, the man who can respect and even marvel at the complexities of nature but without confusing complexity with mystery. The same perspective was already firmly established in Aristotle's time in Hellenic medicine. Consider, for example, a passage from Hippocrates in which a disorder found among the Scythians is under discussion:

> Now the natives put the blame on to Heaven, and respect and worship these creatures (the sufferers), each fearing for himself. I too think that these diseases are divine, and so are all others, no one being more divine or more human than any other; all are alike, and all divine. Each of them has a nature of its own, and none arises without its natural cause.[2]

This is a thesis that could well have appeared in the *Posterior Analytics* and that does appear in one form or another in Aristotle's biological and ethological treatises. But how does it stand in relation to pre-Socratic and Socratic teaching when applied to the soul?

A defensible answer to this question is unavoidably truncated. This is so partly because of the misleading translation of *psyche* as "soul," and partly because Aristotle's developed Psychology is not *psych-ology.* For Aristotle, the term *psyche* is intended to denote that principle as a result of which any living thing comes to have life. He defines *psyche* in his *On the Soul* as the first principle of living things—the *arche zoon*—and regards it therefore as coextensive with the plant and animal kingdoms. The science that would

---

1. The claim that the attribute (and attribution) attaches to all animals *as such* makes clear that sensation is not an accidental but a necessary aspect of what it means for anything to be an animal.
2. This passage is found in section xxii of *Airs Waters, Places,* in vol. 1 of *Hippocrates,* translated by W. H. S. Jones, for the Loeb Classical Library. A slightly different translation is provided and discussed by Arnold Toynbee in his essay, "History," in *The Legacy of Greece,* pp. 306–307.

understand the nature of this principle is different from and more general than what now goes under the heading of "psychology." Moreover, what now does go under this heading, at least as regards *human* psychology—cannot itself be reduced merely to the principles of animation. This will be discussed at length later and in succeeding chapters. The important proposition to establish at this point is that a science of *psyche* for Aristotle is not a version of Aristotle's human Psychology, or what may be called his science of human nature. Indeed, the latter arises from just those aspects of human character that are not assimilable to *psyche* alone.[3] What must be resisted is the temptation first to acknowledge the wide separation between the Aristotlelian *psyche* and the modern sense of the term, and then, on the strength of this distinction, to conclude that Aristotle has no science with which to address the latter.

The pre-Socratic and Socratic philosophers had bequeathed controversial ontologies and had thus created tantalizing epistemological problems. To be sure, the very terms "pre-Socratic" and "Socratic" suggest a uniformity of belief where one actually finds diversity and ambiguity. Still, the overarching ontological issue then (as now) pertains to the basic kinds of "stuff" comprising reality itself. The Homeric world had made room for both matter and spirit, though most of the explanatory work in the epics is achieved by naturalistic-physicalistic theories. Thus is the immortality of the gods attributed to their having *ichor* instead of blood, and thus are nearly all of the hidden forces of nature personified in tangible deities. Even Hades is occupied by visible shadows that can be reanimated briefly by the blood of freshly killed sheep, as is told in Book xi of *Odyssey*. Nonetheless, it is in this same Book that Odysseus learns from Antikleia that his wife and son still wait for him in Ithaka. He longs to hold his dead mother standing before him but, "three times she fluttered out of my hands like a shadow or a dream, and the sorrow sharpened at the heart within me" There is, then, behind the physical appearances a mysterious and immaterial reality, a spirit-world that has the gift of prophecy and clairvoyance; one that can be, as it were, known but not touched by the living.

3. Hugh Lawson-Tancred offers an informing and illuminating discussion of this matter, in his Introduction to *Aristotle: De Anima (On the Soul)*. As he makes abundantly clear, Aristotle does not address what would now be regarded as "the problem of mind" in *De Anima*, nor does he seem to recognize the issues that would torment Descartes and those in his patrimony. But this, though true of *De Anima*, is less the case with those other works in which Aristotle's developed human psychology is to be found.

This ambiguous division between the realm of spirit and the realm of matter is fully honored in the Socratic dialogues and is central to the theory of *psyche* developed in the most scientific of them, the *Timaeus*. It is here that Timaeus gives expression to what seems to be the more or less settled position Socrates reached on the matter. The human *psyche* has a dual existence, the one sublime and the other profane. Earthly life is a saga of torment and temptation, the divine side of human nature held hostage to animal appetites. Anything known at this level of psychic function is shifting and, in the ultimate sense, *unreal*.

The pre-Socratic "nature" philosophers by and large excluded mystery from their sciences and labored instead to develop schemes for reducing *perceptible* reality to its barest physical elements. Heraclitus argued that all reality at base was fire; Thales that it was water; Anaximenes that it was air; Democritus that it was atomic. But Anaxagoras taught that it was reason *(nous)*. And Parmenides, in his lost poem *On Nature*, is led by a goddess to the truth that all *real* existence must be unchanging and eternal, and therefore inaccessible to the (changeable) senses. Over and against the monistic materialism of the physicalists, Anaxagoras, Parmenides, and others set a kind of spiritism or *idealism* that would stand at the foundation of the teachings of the Socratics.[4]

Aristotle's conclusions on this issue are to be considered later, but it can be noted here that his approach to the issue is dramatically different from everything that went before him. Again, it is the *Posterior Analytics* that sets the stage: "The things we seek are equal in number to those we understand. We seek four things: the fact, the reason why, if it is, what it is" (Book II, 89^b 22–24).

Smith reports seeing a centaur. It can be asked whether he saw such a thing, why he saw it, if there are, in fact, centaurs, and what sort of thing a centaur is. There is an important distinction to recognize between the first and the third items on this short list; the distinction between the *subject* of human understanding and its *object*. Even opinions and bare beliefs may be included under the heading of the facts to be accounted for or understood, but from this it does not follow that there are really existing entities corresponding to such opinions or beliefs. Note, then, that from one's having a conception of, for example, centaurs and ghosts, it would

---

4. For an important discussion of pre-Socratic philosophy, consult Jonathan Barnes, *The Pre-Socratic Philosophers*. See also Leonardo Taran, *Parmenides*.

not follow that such entities exist. But in what sense does *psyche* exist, and to what extent does it challenge or support the premises of monistic materialism? These questions lead to an examination of Aristotle's critique of earlier theories of *psyche* and to an analysis of his conceptions of substance, form and matter.

The most general criticism Aristotle directs at earlier theories is that they often fail to raise the right general questions, and they fail as well to consider some of the most obvious facts arising from a study of the world of living things. They are, then, theories that are either indifferent to empirical modes of confirmation or mistaken in their attempts at such confirmation. In a word, Aristotle's predecessors—from his perspective—just got things all wrong, chiefly because they failed to specify what sort of entity the soul must be in order to account for the facts that needed explaining; or they postulated incorrect properties of the soul on the mistaken assumption that such properties were necessary to account for the alleged functions of the soul. Seldom did they ask any of the fundamental questions that should guide inquiry in such an area. To wit: Is the soul a potentiality or an actuality? Is it a substance, a quale, a quantum? Whatever it is, is it the same sort of entity in a horse, a dog, a man, and a god? Does it have parts? Is it part of the body and, if not, is it related to the body?[5]

If the central questions that inspired pre-Socratic and Socratic investigations of the soul pertain to the facts of *movement* and *sensibility* in the world of the living, correct answers will not arise from a defective understanding of movement *qua* movement. A sound biology must be erected on a sound physics, as it were.[6] This leads directly to the celebrated and pivotal form/matter dichotomy recognized as being at the foundation of Aristotle's theory of the soul.[7]

5. All of these questions are set forth right at the outset in *On the Soul* (402ª 10–402ᵇ 5).

6. In his detailed introduction to his own translation of *On the Soul*, Hugh Lawson-Tancred notes that the theory of the soul developed in *De Anima* "is an exercise in what may be called Meta-biology" (p. 48). Actually, it is metabiological and also biological. He goes on to say that in this and Aristotle's other psychological works, one will not find concern with or anticipations of the problem of consciousness or the possibility of the soul's immortality. Thus, "for anyone for whom these questions are what the problem of the soul 'is about', the *De Anima* will seem very much Hamlet without the Prince" (p. 49). As noted in the current and later chapters, I regard this view as misleading and perhaps even incorrect. The problem of consciousness need not be confined to Cartesian versions, and it retains its Cartesian stripes even when presented as the problem of *sensation*. Nor must the question of the soul's immortality be christened in order to be counted among the topics of importance in a philosopher's works. Here, however, I anticipate my final chapter.

7. Discussions of the dichotomy yield one of the thickest chapters in Aristotle scholarship. Important recent contributions have informed but not anticipated the analysis set

The last words have not been pronounced on "the" Aristotlelian sense of such key terms as Form *(eidos)* and Substance *(ousia)*, and because of this, there is ample room for speculation as to just what Aristotle had in mind when claiming in several places that the form and the matter of a thing are separable. At a superficial level of analysis, the distinction and the possibility of separation can be illustrated thus:

1. The Trojan horse is made of wood.

2. The Trojan horse can be dismantled, all of its material components set to one side.

3. With 2 completed, there is no longer anything answering to the description, "the Trojan horse."

4. All of the *matter* once comprising the Trojan horse remains.

5. All of the matter once comprising the Trojan horse has now been reassembled to constitute the *eidos*, "the wooden house."

Is this the sense, then, in which Aristotle intends *eidos* to be understood when he states that the soul is the form of the body? Clearly not, and for reasons that tend to be obscured by the painstaking dissections of some recent scholarship. Aristotle would not have tarried to compose a monumental treatise on the soul if every aspect of its nature were mirrored in the behavior of physical things. Indeed, to treat the soul as something compatible with 1 through 5 above is to subscribe to a species of *atomism* that Aristotle was at pains to examine and reject.

What is most salient about the animal kingdom—and especially the larger and complex animals that Aristotle studied—is *activity* and flexible adaptation in contrast with passivity and the invariance of causal sequences. Book θ of the *Metaphysics* offers these difficult but illuminating passages:

> As all potentialities are either innate, like the senses, or come by practice, like the power of playing the flute . . . those which come by practice or by rational formula we must acquire by

---

forth in the text. Of special note among these recent contributions are Lawson-Tancred, *Aristotle: De Anima;* Jonathan Barnes, *Aristotle;* J. L. Ackrill, *Aristotle the Philosopher.* Examples are borrowed and adapted to the objectives of the present chapter, though somewhat different conclusions are reached.

previous exercise, but this is not necessary with those which are not of this nature and which imply passivity . . . [T]he former potentialities must be in a living thing, while the latter can be both in the living and the lifeless; as regards potentialities of the latter kind, when the agent and the patient meet . . . the one must act and the other be acted on, but with the former kind this is not necessary. (1047^b 31–1048^a 8)

Entities possessed of *psyche* are just different from everything else, not only actually but potentially. The events in what may be called the psychobiological sphere involve organisms which, when sufficiently complex, provide *actions* and not merely reactions. The behavior is not explicable solely in terms of cause-effect regularities. Rather, it becomes necessary to consider the entire history of the organism; its innate and acquired modes of adaptation; the part played by its behavior in the overall success of the organism and its species; the role of desire or need or motivation in bringing about one course of action instead of another, where, in fact, both are possible.

Aristotle then goes on to note that *complete actions* are those in which the end itself is included. The act of thinking, for example, is one in which the act itself is of just the same sort *in the process* as it is in the completion. Thus, *thinking* and *having thought* are akin, whereas *learning* and *having learned* are not. So, it is not true that at the same time we are walking and have walked . . . but it is the same thing that at the same time has seen and is seeing, or is thinking and has thought. The latter sort of process, then, I call an actuality, and the former a movement" (1048^b 30–34).

It is only after he has made these distinctions (between actualities and movements, and between the potentialities inhering in living things and those that inhere in dead matter) that Aristotle sets forth his entirely *nonreductive* biology and, in the process, the scheme that will permit a fuller understanding of his nonreductive theory of *psyche*. Here is the much quoted passage:

(I)s *earth* potentially a man? No—but rather when it has already become *seed*, and perhaps not even then . . . E.g., the seed is not yet potentially a man; for it must further undergo a change in a foreign medium. But when through its own motive principle it has already got such and such attributes, in this state it is already potentially a man, while in the former state it needs another principle, just as earth is not yet potentially a statue, for it must change in order to become bronze. (1049ᵃ 1–18)

Earth is not potentially man, for earth *qua* earth lacks that motive principle (in this case, *psyche*) that is necessary for the actualization of man. Even the germinal seed fails to qualify, for in and of and by itself it will not yield man as an actuality. A man decomposed into his elemental material constituents is no longer potentially a man, whereas the same is not the case with, for example, the Trojan horse. The role of *psyche* is not a species of material causation and is therefore not reducible to any set of merely physical attributes. But the role itself is not independent of the specific enmattered entity whose *psyche* it is. The category "Man" refers to entities having a certain defining *eidos*, but here the term is not just morphological. Coriscus is a man in a way entirely different from the way Coriscus is musical.[8] The latter property is acquired, is not built into the very essence/substance *(ousia)* of "man," and is to be understood therefore as a *movement*, not an *actuality*. Coriscus might not have been musical or, having developed his musicianship, might one day lose it, all the while remaining a man. If, then, in some way that remains to be worked out, *the soul is the form and the body is the matter* of Coriscus, the Coriscus who survives the loss of musicianship must retain the identifying *eidos* even as his moving parts, as it were, undergo continuous modification.

What, then, is to be understood by *form*, which clearly goes beyond notions of shape, even as it avoids cousinship with the Platonic version? The answer has to be culled from different trea-

---

8. The example is taken from the *Posterior Analytics* 85ᵃ 25. As I hope to have made clear at this point, Aristotle's analysis may be less complex—and therefore less subject to logical or conceptual defects—than recent scholarship would suggest. A bronze statue could be recast as, for example, a bronze paperweight, the matter in this case surviving unchanged, but the form now entirely different. Professor Ackrill finds no such analogue where the body-soul dyad is involved, and devotes careful thought to unravelling what Aristotle had in mind. (J. L. Ackrill, "Aristotle's definitions of *psyche*," in Barnes et al., eds., *Articles on Aristotle*, 4:65–75.) Jonathan Barnes, in the same volume, argues that man is body-and-soul, "not as a motor-car is made from engine and coachwork, but rather as motor-car with its engine running is 'made from' the running and the works" ("Aristotle's concept of mind," in *Articles on Aristotle*, 4:33.) But for Aristotle there just is no man or animal or plant without *psyche*, so the absence of such simply returns things to the inanimate realm of mere matter. Thus, the question never *can* arise as to what sort of man or beast it is once the soul is no longer present. It would be like asking what sort of bachelor Smith is now that he is married! On the whole, the analysis offered by Hugh Lawson-Tancred seems preferable in the circumstance (Lawson-Tancred, *Aristotle: De Anima*, pp. 59–68), though not without some reservations.

tises in which the *eidos* is recognized as variations around a central, if illusive, theme. In the *Posterior Analytics,* it is claimed that forms are the central subject of mathematics (79^a 7), but in the *Physics,* it becomes clear that "form" for the natural scientist is not the forms considered (abstractly) by mathematicians.

> How far then must the student of nature know the form or essence? Up to a point, perhaps as the doctor must know sinew or the smith bronze (i.e., until he understands the purpose of each); and the student of nature is concerned only with things whose forms are separable indeed, but do not exist apart from matter. . . . The mode of existence and essence of the separable it is the business of the first philosophy to define. (*Physics* 194^b 10–15)

For the mathematician, the *eidos* of the rectilinear triangle is $a^2 + b^2 = c^2$, which is separable in fact from any given (material) instance of right triangles. But for the natural scientist, it is only *enmattered* form that is to be studied and understood. The nature of *essences*—of the very *eidos* of being apart from any considerations of materiality—is the subject not of natural science but of metaphysics.

But later on in the same treatise, *eidos* is presented as nothing less than the final cause or the *that for the sake of which* a given thing is what it is. It is a nonnatural source of movement and change, though it has no principal of motion within itself. It causes movement without itself moving. It is the "primary reality, and the essence of a thing" (198^b 1–3; 199^a 31–33). It is not material itself and is therefore not observed *in* the thing or its parts. It is, alas, the purpose of the thing and,

> It is absurd to suppose that purpose is not present because we do not observe the agent deliberating. Art does not deliberate. If the ship-building art were in the wood, it would produce the same results by nature. If, therefore, purpose is present in art, it is present also in nature. (*Physics* 199^b 27–30)

None of this prevents *eidos* from being no more than the shape of a thing—the *eidos* of the doughnut is still a disc with a hole in the center—for, as Aristotle put it simply, "the container pertains to form and the contained to matter" (*On the Heavens* 312^a 12). Yet, the simpler renditions can be misleadingly simple. Note that the very purpose of a container is to *contain*, and thus its form and essence are at one with the that for the sake of which.

The distinction between Form and Matter becomes more pressing as Aristotle attempts to develop a natural science of living things, a *psych*-ology. In his *Parts of Animals*, he makes clear in the first book that anatomical research is not an end in itself, and that the scientist's task is not confined to a study of the parts of animals *qua* parts. He states specifically that it is not the material composition of the structures that counts, "but rather the total form," just as the study of architecture concerns itself only in passing with bricks and mortar (*Parts of Animals* 645ᵃ 26–645ᵇ 1). Bricks and mortar are the undifferentiated "stuff" of buildings and, although they precede buildings in time, it is (logically) *for the sake of* the buildings that bricks and mortar are fabricated.

This is weakly analogous to the processes governing the development of animals. There is first (in time) the presence of homogeneous biological material (e.g., flesh, bone); but the process of development makes use of these to form the heterogeneous structures (e.g., face, paws) that comprise the very form of an animal and establish its identity. Here, then, the homogeneous is *for the sake of* the heterogeneous. To use the more modern terminology, one would say that undifferentiated masses of cells become increasingly more differentiated and specialized during ontogenetic development. As the course of differentiation and specialization nears completion, a definite set of vital functions becomes possible. The normal adult *form* of the animal is thus attained, all of its diverse functions now understandable as being for the sake of its sensitivity, locomotion, nutrition, etc.

This is all discussed in Book II of *Parts of Animals*, where Aristotle also presents the infamous "heart" theory that would so please his later critics. One must approach the theory with caution. It is only in his *Movement of Animals* that Aristotle suggests that the *psyche* is *in* the heart (703ᵃ 37), but this has led some to regard his general theory as reductionistic. That this is not the case is clear in many of his treatises. Even in *Movement of Animals*, he appears to be offering no more than a hypothesis as to the locus at which converging psychic forces influence the locomotor processes.[9] Thus,

9. It is neither possible nor necessary to reconcile Aristotle's heart-based theory of psychobiology with the facts and principles of the neural sciences. Clearly, the Hippocratics were correct in their speculations regarding the functions of the brain, and Aristotle was wrong. Nonetheless, he was misled as a scientist would be misled, especially one who was in the clutches of a jejune Baconianism. He rejects the propositon that the brain is the seat of the sensations, for example, on the grounds that the brain itself is entirely without feelings of any kind (*Parts of Animals* 656ᵃ 24). In her translation of—and most interesting

in *Parts of Animals,* his exquisite anatomical skills, exercised in the absence of even the rudiments of a science of physiology, actually and understandably misled him. He records the fact that there are "channels" connecting both eyes and both ears to the brain, but that the regions receiving these are themselves bloodless. The channels, however, do make contact with major blood vessels in the brain (656[b] 8–27). Having subscribed to the plausible theory that vital functions depend upon a rich supply of healthy blood of the right temperature, he was then led to conclude—from the most obvious features of vertebrate anatomy, (and not to mention that it is in the chest that *thymos* and *lyssa* are felt)—that this supply arises in and returns to the heart. Accordingly, the heart becomes central to his theory of *psych*-ology. He was, of course, hopelessly misguided in this, but the defect is confined to the jots and tittles of an ancient physiology that must not be expected to come any closer to modern physiology than the atomism of Democritus comes to quantum physics! His mistake was a *scientific* mistake.

For the philosopher who insists that what is knowable is the kinds of questions that can be asked, each of the facts of anatomy —the blood, the bones, the brain, the heart—raises that most basic of questions: *What is it for?* "All animals that have hairs on the body have lashes on the eyelids," except for the Libyan ostrich, and, "This exception will be explained hereafter" (*Parts of Animals* 658[a] 12–16). Why? What is this for, and how is this seemingly pointless coincidence finally to be understood *scientifically?* Man is the only creature with lashes both above and below the eyes. Why? The reason is that lashes (and hair in general) are for protection. Man is erect, his eyes thus being equally vulnerable from above and below. Lashes being *for* protection, the best arrangement is set by nature to achieve this end.

There is, then, a kinship of sorts between form and function, between form and final cause, between form and substance. Aristotle is under no greater burden to employ *eidos* univocally than *form* is employed in English. But when *eidos, telos,* and *ousia* are used more or less interchangeably, an important thesis is asserted. Metaphysical subtleties aside, the world of the biologist is filled

---

essays on—*De Motu Animalium,* Martha Nussbaum draws the conclusion that Aristotle in fact did locate *psyche* within the heart. There is ample room for disagreement here, but I share the position taken by D. M. Balme (1982) against Professor Nussbaum in his review of her book.

with identifiable creatures who can be categorized according to certain family resemblances as regards salient powers and potentialities. Such entities are *substances* in their particularity, and with a form that qualifies them as a such-and-such. It is, however, also part of the very essence of a such-and-such to do such-and-such, want such-and-such, flourish only under such-and-such conditions. Accordingly, the entity *as substance* is actualized, its heterogeneous parts integrated and functioning in a manner conformable to their various purposes.[10] When these heterogeneous parts are considered, it is only to elucidate their role in promoting the overall interests of the animal. As Aristotle prepares to examine the gross anatomy of the heads of animals, he begins this way: "Let us now consider the character of the material nature whose necessary results have been employed by rational nature for a final cause" (*Parts of Animals* 663ᵇ 23). And he quickly adds, "But in all our speculations concerning nature, what we have to consider is the general rule; for that is natural which applies either universally or for the most part" (663ᵇ 28).

Such passages are not to be interpreted too literally. It is a common mistake to regard Aristotle's biological writings as being so uncompromisingly "teleological" as to stand as a kind of self-parody. As it happens, in most of the expected places, Aristotle is quite ready to acknowledge that many anatomical nuances are not for the sake of anything, and are to be regarded as mere exceptions to an otherwise valid general law. His discussion of the gall bladder is illustrative. He does not correctly report the function of this organ or of the bile it contains, but he does note that bile found elsewhere within the viscera is "not for the sake of anything," and that "though even the residua are occasionally used by nature for some useful purpose, yet we must not in all cases expect to find such a final cause" (*Parts of Animals* 677ᵃ 14–17).

The subtle metaphysics returns to haunt this naturalistic formula only when the *separable* aspects of an entity are considered. There is, for example, something essential that makes Socrates the man he is; something quite distinct from his (heterogeneous) anatomical parts, his current health. There is some core-character, the Socrates who remains the same whether seated or standing, thinking or sleeping. There is something that makes Socrates the man

10. Jonathan Barnes concludes that "substance" for Aristotle is a "robustly commonsensical" notion, referring to "perceptible things—middle-sized material objects . . . with which science principally concerns itself" (*Aristotle*, p. 46).

he is, just as there is something that makes human beings *human*. Take this away from an entity and the entity ceases to be what it is; retain it, and the entity remains what it is.

One word that does this metaphysical (and even taxonomical) work for Aristotle is *ergon*, the pedestrian meaning of which is simply one's business as in, "Dentistry is Dr. Smith's *ergon*." But in his ethical works, Aristotle declares reason to be man's *idion ergon*; i.e., man's *distinct business* which clearly refers to something loftier than a career or occupation.[11] And so, a composite picture of a "such-and-such" begins to take shape. Things in the world are knowable in that their (material) existence can be empirically verified and their (essential) identifying functions and powers (scientifically) discerned. Mere matter has form in one sense, but it is form that could be assembled to fashion an indefinitely large number of such-and-such things. The pre-Socratics' attention to, e.g., earth or air or fire was misdirected, therefore, because a scientific understanding of the things of the world cannot arise solely from an examination of their material composition.

This is but a starting point. The scientist moves from the bare facts of matter to an examination of function and of office. What is this such-and-such, what is it for, what is its proper business? Why is it the way it is and not some other way? If the entity is a fit subject for scientific study, then all of its identifying features— *eidos*, *telos*, *ousia*, *ergon*—are thoroughly enmattered and are thus instantiated in a given material being. In biology, it is just the functioning organism that presents these features, and there is no more to *psyche* than what can be observed within and about the organism itself. Aristotle erases all doubt on this point when he states,

> For there is no such thing as face or flesh without soul in it; it is only homonymously that they will be called face or flesh if the life has gone out of them, just as if they had been made of stone or wood. (*Generation of Animals* 734^b 24–26)

Whether a part or the organism as a whole is considered, the possession of *psyche* is established by evidence of function, purpose, and the several offices of life.

"Nature," says Aristotle, "proceeds little by little from things

11. For a fuller discussion of this, consult Thomas Nagel, "Aristotle on Eudaimonia," *Phronesis* (1972), 17:252–259, which is reprinted in Amélie Oksenberg Rorty, ed., *Essays on Aristotle's Ethics*.

lifeless to animal life in such a way that it is impossible to determine the exact line of demarcation, nor on which side thereof an intermediate form should lie" (*History of Animals* 588^b 4–6). His science of ethology is grounded, then, in a theory of emerging complexities, beginning with lifeless matter and leading imperceptibly to the earliest manifestations of *psyche*. The structures as well as the habits of all of the advanced animals conform to the prevailing environmental pressures, and are designed to promote successful breeding, food-gathering, and the rearing of the young (*History of Animals* 596^b 21–30). As is the case with human beings, animals tend to change habitats with the changing seasons. They build or find shelter, nurture and teach their young, fight for their turf, enter into communal affiliations. Some, like the tessellated animals, are spare drinkers. Serpents crave wine and eels can live only in clear water. Elephants can eat no more than nine medimni of barley at one feeding and, as a rule, those birds with crooked talons and flat tongues are inclined to mimicry. Rockfish pair off not only for mating but also for hibernation. Of the animals, only man is spared madness when bitten by a rabid dog. Horses out at pasture suffer only from diseases of the feet, but those reared in stalls are vulnerable to the full range of disorders. Insects die if covered with oil. The elephant's diarrhoea can be relieved by warm water and a mixture of honey and fodder. As a rule, animals are at their wildest in Asia and display the greatest diversity in Libya—"Always something fresh in Libya" (*History of Animals* 606^b 20)—and this, because of climatic factors.

The account offered in *History of Animals* is perhaps the most thorough, detailed, systematic, and objective treatise in ethology ever composed, displaced if at all only by the monumental works of Charles Darwin. It includes summaries of the conditions promoting health and disease in the various species, the minute nuances of digestion, reproduction, ambulation, sleep, gestation, social interaction. Species and genders are compared as regards their perceptual, emotional, and intellectual powers. There is such a welter of fact that an army of naturalists could devote a productive career to the task of confirmation. At the present time, with its well-developed capacity for indignation, Aristotle's review of gender differences in the animal kingdom may be regarded as more offensive than erroneous (608^a 19–608^b 17). But these same passages are followed by descriptions of inter-species rivalries that could have been drawn from a modern textbook in sociobiology. And, although due consideration is given to instinct, the text is punctuated with such enlightened qualifications as, "One may go so far as to say that if there were no lack or stint of food, then those animals that are now feared and are wild by nature would be tame towards man and in like manner toward one another" (*History of Animals* 608 [b] 28–30).

There are, to be sure, mistakes in Aristotle's ethological survey; mistakes of a factual nature and mistakes of a more general conceptual nature.[12] Yet, even these very often fall into the category of the arguable. He credits birds with an intelligence closely approximating that of man, but it is clear that the "intelligence" in question is of the mother wit variety. It is not the vaunted *epistemonikon* that will figure centrally in Aristotle's theory of human rationality. Rather, many species of birds display a number of the architectural, social, and domestic proclivities that characterize human communities. From a strictly empirical perspective, therefore, such commonalities reflect a common underlying *natural* intelligence. It is in the same way that Aristotle's designation of the ant as "most industrious" should be understood, or those "sentinels" of the bee hive. The attributions are based upon observations of *behavior*, and the position taken is that functionally equivalent patterns of behavior arise from what must be functionally equivalent underlying processes. Accordingly, one may use the word *digestion* to cover those events engaged by the ingestion of food and leading to growth and health, even though different species may have different digestive anatomies and mechanisms. Note, then, that the account is everywhere informed by considerations of the *that for the sake of*

---

12. D'Arcy Thompson's old lesson must always give pause to those who would find innocent ignorances in Aristotle's biological treatises. A lengthy quote is in order:

"The reproduction of the eel is an ancient puzzle, which has found its full solution only in our own day. . . . Professor Grassi, who had a big share in elucidating the whole matter, tells us the curious fact that he found Sicilian fisherman well acquainted with the little transparent larva (the *Leptocephalus* of modern naturalists), that they knew well what it was, and that they had a name for it—*Casentula*. Now Aristotle, in a passage which I think has been much misunderstood . . . tells us that the eel develops from what he calls *ges entera*, a word which we translate, literally, the 'guts of the earth', and which commentators interpret as 'earthworms'! But in Sicilian Doric, *ges entera* would at once become *gas entera;* and between 'Gasentera' and the modern Sicilian 'Casentula' there is scarce a hairbreadth's difference. So we may be permitted to suppose that here again Aristotle was singularly and accurately informed; and that he knew by sight and name the little larva of the eel, whose discovery and identification is one of the modern triumphs of recent investigation." ("Natural Science," in *The Legacy of Greece*, pp. 149–150) *which.* It is only in this way that, for example, the actions of birds and of men may be described as *creating shelter*. The bee whose conduct reliably signals threats to the hive is, by the same standard, a *sentinel*.

Even the instinctual predispositions of animals are not immune to environmental and social conditions.

> Just as with all animals a change of action follows a change of circumstance, so also a change of character follows a change of action. . . . Hens, for instance, when they have beaten a cock in fight, will crow like the cock . . . [and] . . . on the death of a hen a cock has been seen to undertake the maternal duties. (*History of Animals* 631 b 5–15)

The psychic principles are life-giving and life-promoting, working together with the natural conditions surrounding the animal. From the smallest larva to the largest mammal the common processes of nutrition, perception, locomotion, and adaptation are evident, but in forms that vary greatly. At this most basic level, the *ergon* of *psyche* is but that constellation adaptive processes that makes possible the survival of the individual organism and the perpetuation of the species. Nature has outfitted her creatures in just this way, and nature's intelligence and purposes are thus as evident in the *psyche* of the cuttlefish as in the rhetoric of the statesman. The soul is the form of the body—but it is, too, the form-as-function of each part of the body. And each species has its identifying forms-as-functions, forms-as-purposes. To know in a scientific way the essential nature of any creature is to know *why* it is the way it is. It is to know what distinguishes it from other forms, and how these distinctions mark it out for a certain *curriculum vitae*.

It is important within this context to address a source of perplexity arising from the seemingly incompatible *philosophy of science* developed in Aristotle's *Posterior Analytics* and the actual natural science presented in the *Parts of Animals* and in the *History of Animals*. In the *Posterior Analytics*, discussed in the previous chapter, Aristotle presents a model of scientific understanding that is grounded in deductive logic and "demonstrative" modes of explanation. Yet, in his naturalistic treatises, the form of inquiry is empirical and the burden of explanation is supported chiefly by description.

Attempts at relaxing this apparent tension have been more common than a healthy skepticism as to its reality.[13] But when Aristotle's natural science, and especially the biological and ethological portions are examined on the whole, their syllogistic and axiomatic character becomes quite evident. There is everywhere the operation of a hypothetical necessity (*Physics* 200ª) of the form: *If* X is the case, then *necessarily* Y must be the case. The framework of his natural science is of precisely this sort, and the teleological features —often included only in passing[14]—serve as reminders of those general laws that operate within the animal economy. Thus, *if* there is to be shelter, then *necessarily* the structure must provide a barrier against wind and rain, etc. And if nutritive processes are to support the health and growth of a creature then necessarily food will be broken down, digested, etc. These relationships are "hypothetical necessities," not in the sense of being arguable or merely speculative but in the sense of not being logically required. After all, shelter is necessary if a creature is to survive, but there is no canon of logic that requires this survival. For all practical purposes, then, the "hypothetical" necessities implicit in the biological treatises are laws of nature (or are laws of nature once removed).

Does all of this make Aristotle's natural science, including his ethology and psychobiology, axiomatic and deductive as per the lessons of the *Posterior Analytics?* Yes, and no. The model of explanation remains syllogistic, whether the topic is Logic itself or the closely kindred subject of mathematics or the very different subject of natural science. A universal law or, in natural science, a highly reliable general law is at the foundation of any scientific understanding of the subject. Particular events are then understood to be instances of the operation of such a law. Accordingly, the eyelashes of quadrupeds are mere and meaningless attributes until they are understood within the larger context of the conditions necessary for the survival of a species. This is the *form* of scientific understanding, and it obtains across subjects. As he states early in his

13. For a lucid discussion and attempted solution of the problem, consult Jonathan Barnes, "Aristotle's theory of demonstration," in J. Barnes, M. Schofield, and R. Sorabji, eds., *Articles on Aristotle*, 1:65–87. Barnes argues persuasively that the method of demonstration represents Aristotle's theory as to how science is to be taught rather than how it is actually to be conducted.

14. See especially W. Wieland's "The Problem of Teleology," pp. 141–160, in Barnes, Schofield, and Sorabji, eds., *Articles on Aristotle*, vol. 1. The following passage is especially instructive: "The effective predominance of the final cause in the explanation of nature results from the fact that in the case of natural things the formal and the efficient causes coincide with the final cause in number or at least in species; and also from the fact that if we speak of a thing we are already by reason of the structure of our language referring to its form" (p. 151).

Progression of Animals, at the start of any inquiry "we must postulate the principles we are accustomed constantly to use for our scientific investigation of nature, that is we must take for granted principles of this universal character which appear in all nature's work" (704^b 12–15). It is just in the nature of the case, however, that for some subjects the ruling principles are exceptionless (universal), whereas for others they are true only on the whole or for the most part. It is to the geometer that one turns for certainties, not to the biologist.

Understood in these terms, Aristotle's ethology is seen to be quite literally a kind of "psychobiology" in that the diverse modes of adaptation at the molar level express the distinctive features of a given species at the more basic levels of anatomy and physiology. Thus, it is in the nature of a given *psyche* that the overall forms and modes of existence are dictated, revealed always and only in those enmattered things that occupy the kingdoms of life. This much of Aristotle's psychology is naturalistic without qualification. Within its framework, human nature is distinct without being exceptional, complex without being mysterious. This will all change only when attention is turned to the *idion ergon* of man.

FIVE

Psychology as a Natural Science: Perception, Learning, and Memory

As noted in the previous chapter, it is the possession of sensations that identifies an entity as an animal. The operation of *psyche* is evident in plants, for they are alive, they reproduce and nourish themselves. But the animal kingdom reflects powers and faculties beyond these, and sensation is not only one of them but is *the* integral feature of all the rest. Alas, "no one can learn or understand anything in the absence of sense" (*On the Soul* 432ᵃ 6).[1] At the very outset, however, it is necessary to recognize the distinction Aristotle draws between perception and *thought*, and thus to anticipate the points at which his overall naturalistic Psychology gives way to a different and special science of *human* nature.

The distinction in question is made in many places and in different ways, but is stated with indubitable clarity in Book III of *On the Soul:*

1. The full implications of this have been traced out most recently by Deborah Modrak in *Aristotle: The Power of Perception.* This important book rescues Aristotle equally from attempts to cast him as a radical materialist or garden-variety dualist. Although the present chapter is indebted to Professor Modrak's careful and systematic analyses, there are notable points of disagreement.

After strong stimulation of a sense we are less able to exercise it than before, as e.g., in the case of a loud sound we cannot hear easily immediately after . . . but in the case of thought thinking about an object that is highly thinkable renders it more and not less able afterwards to think of objects that are less thinkable: the reason is that while the faculty of sensation is dependent upon the body, thought is separable from it. (429ª 31–429ᵇ 4)

In a word, the study of sensation and perception is neither the same as the study of cognition nor readily propaedeutic to it.[2] A celebrated passage from the same Book III of *On the Soul* makes a kindred point, but in a way that admits of various interpretations:

Actual knowledge is identical with its object: in the individual, potential knowledge is in time prior to actual knowledge, but absolutely it is not prior even in time. It does not sometimes think and sometimes not think. When separated it is alone just what it is, and . . . is immortal and eternal (we do not remember because, while this is impassible, passive thought is perishable); and without this nothing thinks. (430ª 20–26)

This passage is extremely important to an understanding of Aristotle's theory of perception and his different theory of abstract, rational thought. The "actual knowledge" that is "identical with its object" is the objectified knowledge gathered by the senses and evaluated by the mind. Perceptual modes of knowing are tied specifically to the senses and, more generally, to the matter that is the body. But the thought that is grounded in perception is *passive* in that the faculty in question receives the gathered information in a manner governed by the mechanisms of perception. Distinct from this, however, is an *active* intellect that yields cognitive ("noetic") knowledge of what is universal *(katholou)* and thus accessible only to mathematical, scientific, and philosophical modes of inquiry and understanding. It is not a species of perception, and it is therefore never discussed at length where Aristotle presents his entirely naturalistic accounts of perception, memory, and learning.[3] It will be examined further in chapter 7.

2. This is one of several grounds on which I take exception to what seems to be the tendency in Professor Modrak's work to conflate perception and cognition. In chapter 5 of my *Systems of Modern Psychology: A Critical Sketch*, the two processes are distinguished along lines that appear to be compatible with Aristotle's theories.

3. A different conclusion is reached by Professor Modrak: "Apart from positing its existence, Aristotle appears to have very little to say about active *nous*. . . . I am inclined to believe that Aristotle in fact shied away from a detailed treatment of active *nous;* forced

Actual knowledge is identical with its object. How is this claim to be understood? The sentence is only grammatically transparent. The Greek text reads, *"To d' auto estin h kat' energeian episteme to pragmati."* The word customarily translates as "object" is *pragma* (dative: *pragmati*) but more than one interpretation is supportable, for *pragma* also figures in, e.g., the "object" of litigation, or in "a matter of no consequence" *(ouden pragma)*. Nor is *episteme*, understood within the context of *energeia*, something that answers unequivocally to "actual knowledge." An *episteme* considered *kata energeian* is also, "the understanding, in relation to its actual operation." What begins to take shape, then, is an assertion to this effect: "The understanding, considered in relation to its actual operation, is just whatever it is that is the object of its concern".

This is by no means an elegant rendering of the passage, and it is not even offered as a more correct reading. Instead, it is designed to produce some hesitation in taking Aristotle's theory of cognition as a "copy" theory of the well-known Humean stripe. As will be discussed, Aristotle's theory of perception is of this stripe; but *aisthesis* is neither *nous* nor *episteme*, and these latter terms are the ones employed by Aristotle at this point.

As the theory of perception is developed in the first two books of *On the Soul*, Aristotle critically assesses earlier theories: radically materialistic theories which consider the soul to be no more than a congeries of very fine elements, and radically idealistic theories that install the soul as the author of all movement and change. Materialism fails on several grounds, not the least of which is the absence of rationality in creatures whose material organization is complex, and the absence of perception and movement in plants which nonetheless possess *psyche* (410^b).

The error earlier commentators committed was the failure to recognize the various expressions of *psyche* and the manner in which these expressions are tied to distinguishable forms of plant and animal life. What must be abandoned are the customary modes of discussing *psyche*, for in these figures of speech can be found the seeds of any number of confusions. Thus, it is mistaken to say that

---

by his general theory of cognition to posit a state of continuous intellectual activity, Aristotle may have realized that this postulate could easily be exploited by dualists—an intuition the subsequent history of philosophy was to bear out" (*Aristotle: The Power of Perception*, p. 127). The case for Aristotle's own version of dualism, hinted at in this current chapter, is made more strenuously in the seventh and final chapters.

the soul grieves, thinks, perceives, or is frightened or angry—statements no different from those that would have the soul also building a house. Rather, it is the person who is able to do such things and be in such states, as a result of having a soul (*On the Soul*, 408 b). Furthermore, there is a difference between those psychic functions that operate through and with the body, and that special psychic entity—reason *(nous)*—which "seems to be an independent substance implanted within us and . . . incapable of being destroyed" (*On the Soul* 408 b 19).[4] In the matter of perception, learning, and memory, however, it is by means of *psyche* that such processes are possible, though it is not *psyche* itself that is properly described as, e.g., seeing or remembering. "It is doubtless better to avoid saying that the soul pities or learns or thinks, and rather to say that it is the man who does this with his soul" (*On the Soul* 408 b 13–14).

What all perceptions have in common is the capacity to take on the forms (without the matter) of the things perceived, a process Aristotle likens to the application of a signet ring to a soft wax (*On the Soul* 424 a 18–23). What the perceptual faculties have that permits such effects are attributes of the same nature as those that are perceived (e.g., temperature, shape, color, mass) and able to take on a wide range of changes in these same attributes. The power of perceptual discrimination arises from the differences between the imposed attributes and the perceptual system's own average value. As a result, sight has not only the visible but also the *invisible* among its proper objects, and the same is true of the other senses. Their effective stimuli are conditions that fall above or below the sense's own average state. Stimuli that perfectly match the system's own condition or state are not perceived (*On the Soul* 424 a 1–15).[5] If an object is to be perceived, there must be an organ capable of taking on its form and accomplishing this by undergoing an alteration of its own form. Plants and inanimate things can be affected by things, but cannot perceive them. Softened wax does not *perceive* the signet ring because, although it takes on the form

4. The text is, *"O de nous eoiken egginesthai ousia tis ouda, kai ou phtheiresthai,"* J. A. Smith reading *nous* here as "thought". With *nous*, then, the soul reflects a state or condition *(ousia)* like no other and is spared the fate of all entirely material functions and processes.

5. It is tempting to modernize Aristotle's views by assimilating them to contemporary principles of sensory physiology. Of the latter, he could not, of course, know anything. But questions of *mechanism* put aside, his theory of perception is clearly a species of equilibrium-theory which requires a disruption of the steady-state as a necessary condition for effective stimulation.

of the ring, it has no relevant internal state whose variations are finally what is sensed.

On the strength of this theory, Aristotle is led to the conclusion that stimuli of roughly comparable magnitudes cannot be discriminated if they are presented simultaneously; nor are clear perceptions possible when objects are presented to persons lost in thought or frightened or otherwise engaged with still other stimuli (*Sense and Sensibilia* 447ᵃ 12–24). Stimuli must vie for representation within a given sense, and the senses vie with each other when stimulated at the same time. The theory implicitly advocates a perceptual process of limited channel-capacity where representation is determined *ceteris paribus* by the magnitude of competing signals and by the level of ongoing activity in each of the sensory systems. Simultaneously presented stimuli are blended in their effects, neither of them individually perceived.

The form of all perception is spatio-temporally continuous, for there is no temporal interval so brief and no spatial magnitude so slight as to be imperceptible. Were it otherwise, a person "would, during such time, be unaware of his own existence, as well as of his seeing and perceiving" (*Sense and Sensibilia* 448ᵃ 25–448ᵇ 12). This is not to say that percipients have quantitatively accurate perceptions of time and space. Nor is it the case that this continuity is veridical: "[A]t times an object of sight appears indivisible, but nothing that one sees is really indivisible" (*Sense and Sensibilia* 448ᵇ 14–15). Rather, Aristotle's theory of perception records a salient fact of experience; viz., its wholeness, unity, and seamlessness. Additionally, there is the recognition that some stimuli (e.g., sounds) take time to reach the percipient and are thus completed before they are experienced. Moreover, the disposition of the sensory systems predispose the percipient to experiences of a certain kind. Thus, "when the fingers are crossed, one object seems to be two; but yet we deny that it is two; for sight is more authoritative than touch" (*On Dreams* 460ᵇ 20–21). There is a hierarchic and judging function that oversees perceptual processes. So even here the theory moves beyond a mere "copy" theory and begins to make room for perception as a constructive, and not merely a receptive, faculty.

Aristotle is careful to distinguish between perception *(aisthanesthai)* and other means by which things are brought into consciousness or before the mind. Sensing, imagining, and thinking are different processes and answer to different descriptions. The perception of individual things, on Aristotle's account, is always true and is a faculty possessed by all animals. Thinking is not possessed by all animals, and neither thinking nor imagination provides invariably true reports (*On the Soul* 427 ^{b} 7–28).

It is not entirely clear in what sense Aristotle regards the perception of the individual items as true. The text is, "e men gar aisthesis ton idion aei alethes," which J. A. Smith reads as, "for perception of the special objects of sense is always free from error.[6] The more literal reading is simply, "for the perception of particulars is always true." But *aisthesis* here can also refer to a bare sensation— an ache, a flash of light, a drum beat—and this sort of experience is always true in that it is an incorrigibile element of awareness. Thus, whenever an event in the external world triggers activity within a sensory organ or system, the resulting sensation is "true" in that it is just the undeliberated response of one material object to stimulation by another. To the extent that the percipient reports only this bare sensation, he cannot be wrong.[7] Understood this way, Aristotle's thesis at this point might be more aptly translated, "Unblended sensations are always veridical," in that they report undistorted objective properties. What renders them true is that the stimulus properties are sensed individually and thus the channel-capacity problem never arises.

All of this seems consistent with Aristotle's overall ethological perspective on sensory function. Nothing in his writings indicates that he regarded human and animal forms of sensations as fundamentally different. Complex creatures, facing the burdens of food-gathering, the rearing of young, the provision of shelter, etc., must have the means (faculties) by which to register the main properties of the surrounding environment and to organize their behavior accordingly. The faculties are not, however, limitless in their powers or infallible in their operation. One constraint is temporal in that a given sensory system cannot process different categories of information simultaneously. Nor is it reasonable to assume that such a system can match or duplicate every possible form that external stimuli display, though it is just this form-matching power that is as the foundation of the very act of sensation. But with such

6. In Barnes, *The Complete Works of Aristotle*, vol. 1.
7. W. S. Hett, in his translation for the Loeb Classical Library edition of *On the Soul*, attempts to clarify the passage with this footnote: "In normal cases if a man sees a red object, it is red" (p. 156). It is doubtful, however, that this can be Aristotle's meaning, unless "normal cases" is a circumlocution for a set of conditions under which the percipient confines reports to the bare, undeliberated, and unexplained *fact* of a sensation.

limitations conceded, Aristotle's theory confers veridicality on those sensations that do fall well within the operational range of the senses.

The faculty of imagination *(phantasia)*, however, is quite different. Sensation is caused by a stimulus and arises from the activity of a sense organ, but imagination operates in the absence of either; e.g., in dreams. Nor is it a species of opinion, for the latter carries with it conviction, whereas any number of creatures with imagination do not possess convictions. Moreover, although "sensations are always true, imaginations are for the most part false" *(On the Soul* 428ª 11). What seems to be the case, according to Aristotle, that sensory events involve patterns of activity (movement) set up by the stimulus. The movement that answers directly to the properties of the stimulus is the (always true) sensation. But this movement becomes the proximate cause of still other activity (movement) within the system; activity which yields sensory-like consequences, but ones not tied to the external objects themselves. Imagination is of this sort. It can exist only in sentient creatures, for it depends upon sensation. Yet, it is not causally connected to objects in the external world, but to sensory activity induced by such objects. This is what gives imagination the attribute of seeming-to-be. But this, too, impels action:

> And because imaginations remain in the organs of sense and resemble sensations, animals in their actions are largely guided by them, some (i.e., the brutes) because of the non-existence in them of thought, others (i.e., men) because of the temporary eclipse in them of thought by feeling or disease or sleep". *(On the Soul* 429ª 5–9)

Imaginations and dreams have much in common, and Aristotle generally explains the two in the same way. In both cases, activity persists in sensory systems long after the removal of the instigating stimulus. Such persistence is the basis for imaginings, for dreams, and for the visual aftereffects produced by long exposure to a moving or a colored stimulus *(On Dreams* 459ᵇ 11–24).

> What happens in these cases may be compared with what happens in the case of projectiles moving in space. For in these cases the movement continues when that which set up the movement is no longer in contact. *(On Dreams* 459ª 28–30)

The theory to this point may be summarized in the following way. Sentient creatures are equipped with organs able to take on the form of external objects and thus produce faithful representations of them internally. The fidelity of the reconstruction or representation extends only to unblended sensations arising from commerce with particulars. The more complex the stimulus—which is to say, the greater the number of simultaneously projected attributes—the more mixed or blended the percept, and, therefore, the less faithful and, indeed, *the less true* the representation. The manner by which external objects produce their effects is kinetic. Movement is initiated in the sensory systems, the movement somehow coding the form of the stimulus. Where the relationship between the object and its effects is isomorphic, the sensation can be said to be *always true*.[8] But the activity in the sensory systems can and does outlast the actual stimulus, and this activity is often so similar to that produced by the stimulus as to be sensibly indistinguishable from it. This activity or movement is the source of *imagination*. Nonrational creatures must react to it as if its contents were real and thus often desirable. Man, through rational reflection, can (but does not always) differentiate imaginings from percepts.

Thought that is independent of concurrent perception is the activity or power by which once-perceived entities are recreated or revived. In order to register the myriad objects of the external world, *psyche* itself must be, as it were, "the place of forms," but have no defining form of its own. The thinking process is not itself a thing or a place, and it has no existence separate from the very act of thinking. Were it a part of the body, then its productions would invariably take on attributes of the body and, furthermore, would not be able to represent still other attributes for which there is no bodily correlate (*On the Soul* 429ᵃ 18–429ᵇ 22). But with imagination and with memory, matters are different. In these cases, the contents are based upon prior perceptions and do arise from a condition of the body; viz., the movements or activities aroused in

8. Deborah Modrak notes the room for misunderstanding created by the word *eikon*. Aristotle certainly requires a *likeness* to exist between the object and its sensory representation, but this need not imply a photographic likeness. As Professor Modrak says, "if A is an *eikon* of B, A must resemble B *in some respect*" (*Aristotle: The Power of Perception*, p. 89; emphasis added). It is clear that Aristotle insists upon an *isomorphism*, perhaps not unlike that proposed by Gestalt psychologists. It is clear, too, that this isomorphism is at least sometimes of the "picture" variety, but sometimes not. It is doubtful that Aristotle subscribed rigidly to any single mode of representation in this connection.

69

the sensory systems by the stimulus. Thus, "if asked, of which among the parts of the soul memory is a function, we reply: manifestly of that part to which imagination also appertains" (*On Memory* 450ᵃ 21).

Having argued for an essentially physiological and kinetic theory of perception and imagination, Aristotle adds a theory of learning and memory that is consistently mechanistic, sense-based, and naturalistic. Stimulation produces patterns of activity within the organism. As is the case in the external world of physical things, so too within animals certain movements naturally produce others. A series of sequential dependencies unfolds such that, in the presence of stimulus A, the organism emits response X. If stimulus A has generally been accompanied by stimulus B, then response X will, in the future, occur in response to A or to B—or, for that matter, to the recollection of either. "Acts of recollection are due to the fact that one movement has by nature another that succeeds it" (*On Memory* 451ᵇ 11) and,

> If this order be necessary, whenever a subject experiences the former of two movements thus connected, it will experience the latter; if, however, the order be not necessary, but customary, only for the most part will the subject experience the latter of the two movements". (*On Memory* 451ᵇ 11–14)

Here again there is a strong *realist* component in the theory. The associational processes within the percipient are such that, where the external conjunctions are necessary, the subject's internal representations are unfailingly conjoined; where, however, the external ties are only customary, the subject has only a strong tendency to associate them.

On the assumption that the movements established by stimulation naturally lead to still other movements, Aristotle's theory of recollection anticipates certain modern principles of serial learning; e.g., that near-associates are more readily recalled than are those more distantly spaced within the series. In attempting to recall something, the best tactic is to begin at a specific point in the series and, as it were, let nature take its course.[9] "For as one

---

9. Although Aristotle's text makes claims about the serial-position effect in memory that appear to be wrong, consult Richard Sorbji's *Aristotle on Memory*, pp. 31–34. Aristotle seems to be saying that it is the middle term in a series that is most easily recalled, whereas modern psychology has established that the earliest and latest terms in a series are most memorable. But Aristotle is referring to the middle position of triplets extracted from a longer series.

thing follows another by nature, so too that happens by custom; and frequency creates nature" (*On Memory* 452^a 30). The frequent conjunction of A and B produces by custom a veritable *natural* association between them, such that B now follows A in thought as if the two were naturally connected.

When the patterns of activity instigated by one stimulus are very similar to those aroused by another, the tendency toward confusion is great. Accordingly, errors in associational learning arise from a process of generalization. As the mind reviews its contents in search of, for example, a name—perhaps in response to an event or a face or something needing to be done—the chain of associations is engaged, but the mental acts are vulnerable to deflection away from the correct chain and to attraction by a different but similar one. "This ... consideration explains too how it happens that, when we want to remember a name, if we know one somewhat like it, we blunder on to that" (*On Memory* 452^b 5–6) This search is one that takes place within the medium of the body; it is the search for an actual image or form or representation.

It is the active nature of this search that distinguishes recollection from memory, and it is for this reason that Aristotle considers recollection to involve an inferential process; i.e., a movement of thought from some current state to another one like it, having occurred at an earlier time and bearing some sort of relation to it. One who strives to recollect is, in fact, striving, and must engage in an investigative activity grounded in inferences. Many animals have the faculty of memory, but "none, we venture to say, except man, shares in the faculty of recollection" (*On Memory* 453^a 8–9). An associational process can equip creatures with memories of things and places; a process that ties odors of a certain kind to feelings of a certain kind, or sounds of a certain pitch to threats of one sort or another. Such creatures thereby come to conduct themselves in a manner consistent with their survival. But from this it does not follow that they have actively recollected the past, or in any way *thought about* the relationships between and among the items stored in memory. Illustrative of this is the behavior of animals toward food. Food odors that are reliably associated with nutritious foods will attract the hungry animal but not the one that is sated. There is no need to assume any deliberative function at work here, for the effect can be explained fully in mechanistic-associational terms. A food comes to attract an animal in virtue of that food's survival-value. The agreeableness of the odor, then, is contingent on this fact and has nothing to do with odor *per se*. However, some odors are inherently agreeable, e.g., the aroma of flowers. Even here the explanation is grounded in considerations of health (*Sense and Sensibilia* 443ᵇ 20–444ᵇ 1). In neither case does the effect require mental exertions or logical inferences. It arises from either customary or innate associations and is made possible by a (noncognitive) faculty of memory.

It is useful here to consider, but only briefly, the manner in which Aristotle's distinctions between memory and recollection are grounded in an implicit theory of consciousness, said by some to be largely absent from his works.[10] For Aristotle, memory and imagination, like dreams and bare sensations, are patterns of activity within the body; *movements* arising from the material transactions between sense organs and items in the external world. Sensations differ chiefly in that they occur *at the time* of stimulation, whereas memories, imaginations, and dreams come about from a persistence of activity after (sometimes long after) the removal of the relevant stimuli. Nothing beyond the biological properties of the faculties in question need be consulted to understand how this takes place, and nothing in the phenomena themselves entails a conscious, striving percipient. This is all explicitly asserted in Aristotle's *Generation of Animals* when he considers the capacities of prenatal and neonatal organisms, including human beings. He notes that it is difficult to determine whether or not there are states of wakefulness during the earliest stages of development, but that sleep can be interrupted even in the fetus during the later stages, a fact that has been established "in dissections and in the ovipara" (*Generation of Animals* 779ᵃ 8–10). He notes also that infants when awake neither laugh nor cry but do both when asleep, this proving that sensations occur in animals and neonatal human beings even during sleep. And, of course, sleepwalkers prove the point completely, and are quick to acknowledge that the sensations taking place during the sleepwalk are not at all dreamlike (*Generation of Animals* 779ᵃ 12–26). All in all, then, it is clear that for both

10. In his introduction to *Aristotle: De Anima*, Hugh Lawson-Tancred insists not only that Aristotle does not have such a theory but fails to recognize places where such a theory would naturally fall. He says, for example, that Aristotle conflates two very different senses of *aisthesis*—one the simple act of perception and the other an operation akin to judgment. "[E]ither of the two concepts . . . could be so treated as to connect with the general problem of consciousness, [but] Aristotle shows no explicit awareness of this possibility" (p. 78). (p. 78).

human and animal creatures sensory processes are active even in the absence of consciousness, deliberation, and understanding.

With *recollection*, on the other hand, the process is initiated by the actor and entails a knowing, striving, *conscious* being. Aristotle draws attention to the active nature of recollection in still another way when he contrasts it with relearning (*On Memory* 452ᵃ 5–13). Sometimes, no matter how long or effortful the search for a forgotten item, recalling it proves to be impossible, and the information must be reacquired. Thus, *relearning* becomes necessary where recollection has failed and where, therefore, the active powers of the person are no longer sufficient for the purpose. It is the *person* who recollects and, when his powers fail, it becomes necessary to reprogram the system. Memory *simpliciter* is a function of the faculty of sense perception (*On Memory* 451ᵃ 17) and is passive in that it is but the revival of likenesses of whatever the senses initially recorded.

Running throughout Aristotle's theory of perception and memory is a concept that has been dubbed "the *Logos* doctrine."[11] As with certain of his predecessors, including Plato, Aristotle takes the domain of the sensible as ranging across a spectrum of values or magnitudes the extreme ends of which yield sensory opposites; e.g., darkness and light, black and white, hot and cold, wet and dry. To be capable of sensation, an animal must have within its sensory apparatus the power to react to events falling along such a continuum of magnitudes. Thus, the sensory processes must have the *potential* to take on or absorb the form of the *actual*. As Aristotle recognized, the percipient in a way "sees" that it is dark; i.e., the percipient *sees darkness*, and this indicates that the extreme of a sensory continuum is not bounded at one end by a nullity, but by an opposite.

The continuum of stimulation is a continuum of magnitudes, and the sense organs themselves are also magnitudes in that they have mass and extension. But sensation itself is not a magnitude.

11. For a full discussion, consult Deborah Modrak, *Aristotle* pp. 56–62. Professor Modrak names it such and notes that it is difficult to grasp (p. 56), and ties it to the opposite-pairs hypothesis. Consult also Jonathan Barnes' interesting comments on *logos* in his *Early Greek Philosophy*, pp. 21–22. He points out that to give a *logos* of something is to explain the thing or supply a reason. On this construal, *"logos* comes to be used of the faculty with which we give reasons, i.e., of our human *reason"* (p. 21). This might support the thesis that regards the *logos* of the perceptual faculty its comprehension of the object as the object really is.

Rather, it is the *logos tis kai dunamis* of things having magnitude (*On the Soul* 424ᵃ 28–29). Now, *dunamis* is a commonly occurring term in Aristotle's works, and it invariably stands for a power or faculty or ability. And, though *logos*, too, is found throughout Aristotle's writings, its meaning in the present context is far from obvious. Translators typically render it as "form," but *eidos* is nearly invariably Aristotle's term for form. Perhaps the more literal meaning of *logos* as "term" or "word" is closer to Aristotle's own meaning. What the faculty of sensation possesses is the potential to respond to a stimulus *in its own terms*, as it were, and thus to convey its form. The senations of hot, cold, warm, etc., are *logoi* of actual objects in the external world. Thus, the way the sensory mechanisms represent the world is pretty much the way the world is, for sensations report the facts of the world in the world's own terms *(logoi)*.

This inevitably raises a question as to the manner in which such *logoi* are compared, contrasted, assimilated. Say, for example, that the eye with its associated functional anatomy reports smoky vapors emanating from the surface of a bowl. At the same time, the sensory organs of the lips record the hotness of the substance in the bowl while the olfactory mechanisms indicate a perfumelike ingredient. Here are three distinct and unconnected phenomena, each of them (on Aristotle's account) faithfully expressing reality in its own terms. How are the accounts pulled together to yield the perception, "hot and spicy soup"? Aristotle's answer is that the percipient possesses, in addition to the five special senses, a unifying and indeed unified faculty that receives and pools the information arising in the special senses. It is not a "sixth sense," for, "there is no sense in addition to the five" (*On the Soul* 424ᵇ 22); thus, there is no special organ mediating its operations. Rather, the task is accomplished by the percipient himself, in whom the data from diverse senses are integrated.

> Each sense then is relative to its particular group of sensible qualities. . . . Since we also discriminate white from sweet, and indeed each sensible quality from every other, with what do we perceive that they are different? It must be by sense; for what is before us is sensible objects. . . . What says that two things are different must be one. . . . Therefore what asserts this difference must be self-identical, and as what asserts, so also what thinks or perceives". (*On the Soul* 426ᵇ 9–23)

The necessary work is accomplished by what Aristotle calls the *common sense (aisthesis koine)*, which is not a separate and distinct sense in itself but a mode of perceptual integration. In the places where he discusses it (e.g., *On the Soul* 425ª 14–425ᵇ 12), this "common sense" not only integrates the data provided by the five special senses, but lessens the deceptions to which they are vulnerable. The properties of bile, he notes, include yellowness and bitterness, the former a proper object of sight and the latter of taste. One might see a yellow fluid and incorrectly identify it as bile, unless one were able to supplement the visual information with, in this case, gustatory information. Again, however, the two classes of information must be pooled in such a way as to produce the combined experience of yellow-colored-bitter-tasting, but the special senses cannot achieve this pooling. It is accomplished by a process that is the common substrate of all distinct experiences. This "common sense" then, as it functions within Aristotle's theory of perception, is no less than the percipient's awareness of his several and distinguishable sensations.

The contention here is that percipients have a reflective power by which they are aware of their own experiences and thoughts. For there to be perception, there must be a percipient.[12] Like thinking, perception has something of an assertoric element that goes beyond the passive stages of sensation. One not only hears; one knows that one is hearing. Perception, then, is something of a dialogue between presented facts and implicit assertions as to their actual properties. The fact in mind is *logos*.

Even at the level of sensation and perception, Aristotle's Psychology begins to detect the limitations of a radical materialism. The flesh, he says, "cannot be the ultimate sense organ: if it were, the discriminating power could not do its work without immediate contact with the object" (*On the Soul* 426ᵇ 15–17). This is not a claim revealing ancient ignorances about the adequate stimulus for sensation. Aristotle could not have known about cells in the olfactory epithelia or electrical events in the hair cells of the basilar membrane. Nonetheless, he knew that odors and sounds do not

12. On this point Deborah Modrak (*Aristotle*, pp. 145 ff.) makes the interesting suggestion that Aristotle's theory of conscious awareness differs from modern notions. She argues that, at base, the presumed order of causation is different, with Aristotle regarding reflexive awareness as arising from the objective relations conveyed by the stimuli themselves. But here, too, much seems to be made of Aristotle's rather offhand comments on the similarity of perception and thinking. They are alike in that they are both assertoric. They are entirely unalike, however, in that thinking can have totally abstract "objects" for its content.

have the properties of tangible things and, therefore, that perceptions of this sort are not mediated by tangible alterations of the flesh. There is in each experience the *logos;* the representation of a stimulus in its own terms. The process of representation must be a kind of *isomorphic* one, else the experience would be a report of the conditions of the sense organs themselves.

Soft wax and signet rings aside, Aristotle's theories of perception, learning, and memory are naturalistic without being atomistic. His is a "common sense" theory of perception grounded in ethological considerations and informed by the most reliable of introspectively yielded facts. The presence of *psyche* in the world introduces a special set of phenomena unheralded by lifeless matter. Aristotle takes these phenomena as he finds them, and attempts to explain their causes scientifically. To account for perception, learning, and memory, little more is necessary than a biological theory based on isomorphic modes of representation and storage. However, the *unity* of experience introduces another order of complexity and requires the addition of the capacity for self-awareness. Still, the theory remains naturalistic and biological, for the objects of perception and learning have not yet risen higher than the level of the things of the world.

In his common sense theorizing, Aristotle was willing to notice a number of similarities between perception, memory, and learning on the one hand, and *understanding* on the other. However, the kinship was of a limited sort and, if extended beyond its proper degree, would lead to error. Perceiving and understanding, he said, are not identical; "for the former is universal in the animal world, the latter is found in only a small division of it" (*On the Soul* 427 ^{b} 8).

SIX

Psychology as a Natural Science: Emotion and Motivation

An examination of Aristotle's theory of emotion and motivation is burdened by the special and "specialized" connotations of these words in contemporary psychology. Aristotle's own systematic Psychology covers the cases modern psychology has in mind, but not always in the same terms. In the Classical Age, the concept of a motive would be expressed most often either by the word *prohairesis*, meaning an intention or purposeful choice, or *aitia*, meaning a causal or predisposing condition. One billiard ball, as an *aitia*, impels another to move when it strikes it. The desire to achieve some end exists as a *prohairesis* within the person and thus makes his course of action predictable and intelligible.

Modern psychology has tended to regard motives as biological states within the organism inclining behavior in one or another direction. The manner in which such motives operate is not of the billiard-ball variety, for the organism's sensibilities are an integral part of the motivational complex. But neither is such a motive a *prohairesis*, for *self-conscious* striving is not assumed. The modern concept, then, is closer to the classical notion of an *appetite (orexis)*, and it is Aristotle's theory of the appetites that will first be considered in this chapter.

In Aristotle's fourfold theory of causation, as has been discussed in chapter 3, the boundaries separating the formal and the final causes are not sharply drawn. Even the formal and the material causes are sometimes reduced to a near synonymy.[1] Within this same theory, the *efficient* cause is the source of change or movement. But as Aristotle teaches in the *Metaphysics* (996[b] 1–25), a different science is needed for the study of the different modes of causation. Movement and change, at least to a first approximation, are therefore in the province of natural science or "physics" broadly conceived. If by *motivation*, therefore, one is concerned with the basis upon which animals (including human beings *as animals*) are impelled to activity, then the physics of motion is the proper starting point.

"All things that are in motion must be moved by something" (*Physics* 256[a] 2). The movement is produced either by a principle of self-movement or by an impinging external body that imparts motion by collision. Thus, "the stick moves the stone and is moved by the hand, which again is moved by the man; in the man, however, we have reached a mover that is not so in virtue of being moved by something else" (*Physics* 256[a] 7–10). Aristotle's example offers the three ubiquitous ingredients of all kinetic phenomena: a thing that is moved, the thing that moves it, and the instrument of motion (*Physics* 256[b] 13–14). The stone is moved by the stick, and the stick's own motion proceeds from the man who, in this case, is the instrumental term in the relationship between the mover and the moved. There is no external body acting on the man and compelling the movement of the stick. Rather, the conditions that result in the movement of the stick are all internal to the actor himself and constitute the power or faculty of self-movement. Some things in the world are so constituted that, by their very nature and character, they can move themselves, and these are "the animal kingdom and the whole class of living things" (*Physics* 259[b] 3–4).

The matter, however, is rather more complicated than this, even at the level of the most elementary activities, as Aristotle is quick to note. There is, after all, movement of and in the animal that does

1. In the *Metaphysics*, for example, the fourfold theory of causation is summarized at 983[a] 26–32, and the "formal" is presented as a *logos* which W. D. Ross renders as a "formula" or "definitory formula." The text itself states only that the question "why," as answered by any causal account, has a reference. Now, *logos* as the referent is just the *term* (e.g., "statue") whose causes are the subject of inquiry.

not arise from the animal-as-instrumentality; e.g., environmental impingements, breathing, growth, decay (*Physics* 259ᵇ). All of the animal's metabolic processes are instances of motion, and these take place in the sleeping as well as in the walking creature. Such motions as these are continuous throughout the life of the animal, and this requires a continuing source of motion. This source,

> ... is either in motion or unmoved: if, then, it is in motion, it will have to keep pace with that which it moves and itself be in process of change, and it will have to be moved by something: so we have a series that must come to an end, and a point will be reached at which motion is imparted by something that is unmoved. Thus we have a mover that has no need to change along with that which it moves. (*Physics* 267ᵃ 25–267ᵇ 4).

Thus, in the *Physics*, Aristotle has laid the foundations for a psychic power or faculty of movement in the animal enabling self-movement and agency. With these foundations laid, he can declare nearly dismissively that theories requiring that *psyche* itself moves are proposing what is not only wrong but impossible (*On the Soul* 405ᵇ 33–406ᵃ 1). What all such theories have in common is that they assume the soul is joined to the body without inquiring further into the very special conditions that must obtain for there to be any relationship at all between *psyche* and *soma*. Clearly, not just any material entity can be endowed with soul, nor does a given psychic faculty go willy-nilly with corporeal entities (*On the Soul* 407ᵇ 14–19). The animate world contains creatures whose matter-plus-form (body-plus-soul) character serves particular ends and expresses one of nature's ultimate designs. Earlier philosophers, Aristotle says, tended to ignore this overarching principle, neglecting the very nature of the body that is ensouled, "as if it were possible, as in the Pythagorean myths, that any soul could be clothed in any body. ... It is as absurd as to say that the art of carpentry could embody itself in flutes; each art must use its tools, each soul its body" (*On the Soul* 407ᵇ 19–26).[2]

Not only is the principle of self-movement scientifically defensible, but so too is that broad psycho-ethological principle that grants to creatures just those faculties or potentialities as their place within the overall design requires. There is a *fitness* principle at

2. The metaphor is a common one. In *On the Soul* at 432ᵃ 1, he expresses it thus: "the soul is analogous to the hand; for as the hand is a tool of tools, so thought is the form of forms and sense the form of sensible things."

work throughout nature, evident in the domain of perception and learning, and no less evident in the movements and the motivations of creatures that do perceive and learn. The possession of *psyche* is what permits certain qualitative and quantitative changes (movements) within the animal. The sensations are a qualitative change, locomotion a quantitative change *(On the Soul* 415 ᵇ 23– 26). Indeed, animals are classified most generally according to these two powers; the power of *discrimination,* which is made possible by sensation and thought, and the power of *initiating movement.*[3] The respective properties of these two powers are compatible. They must be fully integrated if the animal is to survive.

All this leads finally to the question of what it is that impels animals to move themselves toward one or another location. The faculty in question cannot be the nutritive, for if nutrition required movement, plants would have such powers of locomotion. Nor is the sensitive faculty the source of self-movement, for some nearly immobile creatures are nonetheless sensitive. Nature endows creatures with faculties for a purpose, and therefore the capacity for self-movement must express yet some other power or condition coherently connected with it. These turn out to be appetite *(orexis)* and thought *(nous),* for it is only on the basis of these that an animals is inclined to move itself in one direction or another *(On the Soul* 432 ᵇ 15–433 ᵃ 21).

The movements thus initiated are best considered as goal-oriented behaviors, for what is produced is not merely a movement in space *(kinetika kata topon),* but movement with an end in view; viz., the end of satisfying some craving. And this fact also qualifies the nature of the *nous* involved. It is not the speculative mind *(logizomenos)* but the practical *(praktikos),* and it is the final operation of the latter that is, in fact, the starting point of all goal-directed activity *(On the Soul* 433 ᵃ 10–21).

In light of these considerations, a question arises as regards the form of explanation best suited to the facts. The animal is, to be sure, a physical system, and those internal events that constitute the biological foundations of appetite are themselves physical. Motivation itself, as understood in the present context, is an entirely natural phenomenon. Yet, Aristotle hesitates to consign it totally

3. The "movement" here is *self-movement,* the text being *kinesis aute,* and generally translated as "local movement." It is to be distinguished from such passive movements as accompany respiration or heartbeats, not to mention those induced by collisions between the animal and external forces.

to the domain of the natural scientist *(phusikos)*. Rather, he says, there is a place here for the "dialectician" *(dialektikos)*. This term, generally translated as "logician" or "debater," should be given a broader extension here. The method of inquiry adopted by the Socratics was the "dialectical," and argumentative method seeking to locate those conclusions that were logically consistent and intelligible; accounts that make sense. What the dialectical method must yield is an account that includes the particular but subsumes it under more general principles, and this is what the "dialectician" in Aristotle's account is called upon to do. A display of *orexis*, witnessed by the natural scientist and the dialectician, therefore, would result in different but compatible explanations.

> The latter would define e.g. anger as the appetite for returning pain for pain, or something like that, while the former would define it as a boiling of the blood. (*On the Soul* 403ª 30–403ᵇ 1)

The scientist is concerned with identifying the material and efficient causes of anger, whereas the dialectician searches for the reason. One who would know the why and the wherefore of anger must be both scientist and dialectician, both observer and reasoner.

Any creature possessing the faculty of sensation must also possess appetite (*On the Soul* 414ᵇ 1). And, as imagination is but the persistence or recurrence of that which was once present in sensation, creatures with appetites also possess imagination. The argument for this is straightforward. Even the most rudimentary sensory function permits the animal the experience of touch, and even if this were the only experience, it would by its very nature be able to yield the sensations of pain and pleasure. Where these sensations exist, so too does the desire to avoid the former and secure the latter. The same is the case with hunger and thirst and all impulses of a life-sustaining nature. The motivation—the impulse to move —is grounded in the sensations of pleasure and pain. It is tied to the most basic needs of the organism. Where the faculty of *praktikos* is also present, the motivation is actually framed by the actor and is part of the actor's self-awareness. Nevertheless, there can be *orexis* without *praktikos*. All animals have appetites, but not all have the *praktikos* that permits the framing of means-ends relationships. A creature can act *for* a purpose without acting *with* a purpose. This point is especially clear in light of the rules of definition and explanation laid down in the *Topics*. One can say that *orexis* is a *property* of animals whereas, for example, learning grammar is a *property* of human beings: "A property is something which does not indicate the essence of a thing, but yet belongs to that thing alone, and is predicated convertibly of it" (*Topics* 102ᵃ 18–19). Those motivations explicated in terms of *orexis* are animalistic. They apply to man-as-animal for they are properties of animals, and man generically is an animal.

Motives as appetites, moreover, are stimulus-bound. Aristotle says that it is not the appetite but *the object of appetite* that actually originates the movement (*On the Soul*, 433ᵃ 27–28). Movement, after all, is toward or away from *something*. There are, however, constraints on appetitive behavior in organisms having a rational faculty. Note, for example, how a person might reject a pleasure at hand for a more distant one of greater value; or how one might ingest foul-tasting medicines in the interest of long-term health. What is clear, however, is that resistance to the demands of the moment is possible only for a creature possessing the sense of time, the awareness of a more propitious future (*On the Soul* 433ᵇ 5–10).

The theory of motivation that emerges from these considerations is psychobiological and naturalistic. All behavior is tied to three specific factors: that which actually originates the movement; the means by which this movement is effected; the entity that is, in fact, moved. What originates the movement is of a two-fold nature. It is the perceived or imagined or deliberated *good*, the object or goal toward which the behavior is directed; and it is also the appetite itself, that state within the organism that is moved and that moves. Finally, that which is moved is just the animal itself or those parts of it employed to escape what is painful or obtain what is pleasant. The body of the animal is simply an instrument or tool used by the appetite to bring about the desired internal states. The states are *felt* states in that pleasure or the cessation of pain is the goal. It is not, however, the sensation or feeling-state that impels the action, but the appetite for such a state (*On the Soul* 433ᵇ 13–30).[4]

4. It is clear that the desired state, being one of pleasure or comfort, is finally a condition answering to certain sensory requirements. As David Ross noted, the faculty of appetite finally is absorbed into that of sensation. (Ross, *Aristotle*, pp. 145–146). But Aristotle himself resists this conclusion in a number of places (e.g., *Nicomachean Ethics* 1139ᵃ 19–20), insisting that sensation, unlike appetite, initiates no action. The thesis that does least violence to Aristotle's own words on this subject is one that gives efficacy to the appetites as originators of movement while acknowledging that certain *feelings* are the goal toward which the actions aim. On a related point, it should be said that, because Aristotle's theory of motivation is, indeed, so naturalistic, it creates a certain problem for that rationalistic theory of moral and social behavior found in his ethical and political writings. As Hugh Lawson-Tancred has observed, "Aristotle never really makes clear whether the concept of desire belongs to psychology or physiology, so that he cannot show how the

Controversy surrounds the question of whether Aristotle's theory of motivation-as-appetite is uncompromisingly materialistic. There is a sequence proposed to cover all (appetitively) motivated behavior; viz., 1) appetite, 2) the object of appetite, 3) movement toward that object, 4) the elimination or attenuation of the appetite. It has been suggested that Aristotle never comes to grips with the burning question of whether or not the appetite itself is exclusively physical, so that the entire "psychology of motivation" might thereby be reduced to a problem for physiologists.[5] As has been seen, however, Aristotle recognizes that a purely scientific account of this sequence can be rendered, but will be incomplete. Nonetheless, his theory of the appetitive motives is intended to be consistent with his theory of perception and, as discussed in the previous chapter, this latter theory is naturalistic and biological. It is just because human beings are at once biological and rational—it is just because of the duality of human nature—that the *objects* of human desire can transcend the realm of creature-comforts. Once this happens, the "psychology of motivation" is no longer confined to appetitive motives but to those that have virtue as their end. As will be made clear in following chapters, the natural scientist necessarily has little to offer by way of explanation at this point.[6] Note, however, that in addition to *orexis* the causes of movement include a species of *nous*. Aristotle does not withhold this faculty from the advanced species, though only man is credited with the power of abstract rationality and the comprehension of universals.[7]

Although the issue is not confronted head on in *On the Soul*, it is examined in the other naturalistic treatises and always in a way tending toward the same general conclusion. In *Movement of Animals*, for example, Aristotle compares animal behavior with the movements of puppets and acknowledges the functional similarities of their respective anatomies. But the puppets undergo no internal *qualitative* change such as that which is the mark of sensation and thought (701ª 2–24). Psychological attributes are not just

---

movement produced by the soul at least in the case of man can justly be called an action, the product of rational and conscious agency" (*Aristotle: De Anima*, p. 211).

5. Hugh Lawson-Tancred, p. 213.

6. It is still true, however, that Aristotle does not directly address this valid question in *On the Soul*. His position, however, would seem to be unambiguous when located within the context of his moral treatises, particularly where the problem of incontinence is under examination.

7. This faculty receives the special name of *epistemonikon* from Aristotle when, in *On the Soul*, he declares it to be never moved, ever at rest (433ª 17).

physical attributes by another name. Appetite as studied by the scientist may be no more than a species of movement within the body of the actor, but it is more than this from the perspective of the actor himself:

> I want to drink, says appetite; this is drink, says sense or imagination or thought; straightaway I drink. In this way living creatures are impelled to move and to act, and desire is the last cause of movement, and desire arises through perception or through imagination and thought. (*Movement of Animals* 701ᵃ 32–701ᵇ 1)

Intelligent, goal-oriented behavior, as emitted by any number of animals, provides evidence of conscious striving. The faculty of *praktikos* is not present in lifeless matter. The faculty of *orexis* arises from the capacity for pain and pleasure. Thus, the entire theory of appetitive motivation is grounded in the assumption of a creature with feeling and awareness, a creature with cravings and longings. At the advanced levels of biological organization, these are the attributes that go along with being *ensouled*. At these levels, the animals must be regarded as endowed with conscious awareness and with the power of acting as intending agents. This is all compatible with a rigidly physiological theory of appetite, but not with a rigidly materialistic theory of *psyche* itself.[8] The animals at this level are, one might say, *psychologically* and not just *psychically* endowed. The animals in question, it is worth noting, include children, "since children in fact live at the beck and call of appetite, and it is in them that the desire for what is pleasant is strongest" (*Nicomachean Ethics* 1119ᵇ 6–7).

But living creatures are moved by any number and variety of conditions and causes. These include thought *(dianoia)*, and imagination *(phantasia)*, purposeful choice *(prohairesis)*, will *(boulesis)*, and lust or craving *(epithumia)*, as summarized in *Movement of Animals* (700ᵇ 4). Accordingly, it finally makes little sense to ask whether each source of movement arises from a different "part" of the soul, or if, because of this multiplicity of factors, the soul has

---

8. It is common for Aristotle to illustrate his concept of the appetites with both human and infrahuman examples, often in the same place within the text. This provides additional support for the claim that his theory of appetitive motivation is grounded firmly in his natural science and thus requires no more than scientific modes of explanation. The advent of abstract rationality in the animal kingdom does not, therefore, alter the essential nature of appetitive motivation, but it dramatically alters its power over the actor. Even without this faculty, however, the behavior of animals is distinguished from that of purely physical systems as the passage from *Movement of Animals* makes clear.

multiple parts. Aristotle's "faculty psychology" is a common sense Psychology that resists the wanton multiplication of faculties.[9] The soul, in one sense "is an infinity of parts" (*On the Soul* 432^a 24), depending on how one chooses to define and catalogue the infinite number and variety of psychic phenomena. The effect of emotion *(pathos)* is also various. It induces movement as a result of the feelings it excites and the states it creates.

The subject of the emotions is, of course, central in Aristotle's ethical writings, specifically in relation to the virtues of justice and temperance. The character of a person is disclosed in part by the objects of his love and anger, the things he longs for and would sacrifice to bring about. The emotions in these contexts work with or against the most elevated forms of rationality and, as will be discussed in the next chapter, are no longer operating in the totally natural and naturalistic domain of man-as-animal. Nonetheless, the emotions *do* operate in this domain and provide further support for that aspect of Aristotle's Psychology that is naturalistic and biological.

One effect of emotional states is simple distraction. As feelings increase in intensity, it becomes ever more difficult for the organism to maintain a clear focus on the perceptual data at hand. There is a strong tendency for these data to be colored or transformed in a manner dictated by the prevailing emotional state:

> We are easily deceived respecting the operations of sense-perception when we are excited by emotions, and different persons according to their different emotions; for example, the coward when excited by fear, the amorous person by amorous desire. (*On Dreams* 460^b 3–5)

Emotions, therefore, do not act uniformly, but relatively. Their effects are chiefly those of amplification; they intensify or energize dispositions that are already in place.

The broadest constitutive description Aristotle offers of the soul is found in Book II of the *Nicomachean Ethics*, where he confines what is found in the soul to three types of entities: Passions, faculties, and states. In the same place, he delineates these as follows:

9. As Hugh Lawson-Tancred observes in this connection, Aristotle's digression here "heralds the end of the 'faculty psychology' bequeathed to the Academy by Plato, and suggests the growing interest in psychological realism that is so strongly to characterize the Hellenistic Age" (*Aristotle - De Anima*, p. 250, n. 128).

> By passions I mean appetite, anger, fear, confidence, envy, joy, love, hatred, longing, emulation, pity and in general the feelings that are accompanied by pleasure or pain; by faculties the things in virtue of which we are said to be capable of feeling these . . . by states the things in virtue of which we stand well or badly with reference to the passions, e.g. with reference to anger we stand badly if we feel it violently or too weakly, and well if we feel it moderately; and similarly with reference to the other passions. (1105^b 20–29)

To stand well or badly is to have a certain disposition *(hexis)* which, for a rational being, is of a very special sort. But animals, too, have natural dispositions of an instinctual variety, and it is not inapt to describe the emotions of a given animal as being "mad" or "vicious."

Now, what a given emotion does to an organism depends further on the faculties possessed by that organism. Creatures with sensory capacities (therefore) have appetites in that they can be pained and thus will have the *orexis* to remove or relieve the pain. With increasing orders of psychological complexity comes a richer variety of conditions capable of eliciting emotional states. Only beings capable of that form of rationality on which justice rests can be *angered by injustice.* It is not, then, entirely the properties of the stimulus or the environmental conditions that determine the emotions, but only how such conditions are mined by the faculties of a creature that has at the time a given predisposition. As Aristotle says in the *Eudemian Ethics,* the moral quality of a being is not established by the presence of anger, fear, or other passions. "Quality does not depend on these—they are merely experienced—but on the faculties," by which he means those features of the actor that qualify him as, e.g., irascible, shameless, courageous, etc. (1220^b 15–20).

The quality or character of a being is not invariably given or instinctive. Animals—unlike the stone that will never learn to fly no matter how often it is thrown in the air—are shaped by instruction. As the very word suggests, *ēthos* is grounded in *ethos;* character arises from custom or habit *(Eudamian Ethics* 1220^a 38–1220^b 5). So, too, are the emotions shaped, as is the power to resist and exploit them. The emotional desires can wreak havoc if unchecked, "for desire is a wild beast, and passion perverts the minds of rulers, even when they are the best of men" *(Politics* 1287^a 30–31), but the skillful rhetorician will employ the language of anger to induce outrage (*Rhetoric* 1408ᵃ 16).

Consistent with Aristotle's comparative psychology, his theory of emotion regards the human emotions as just the more sharply delineated forms of what is found among all the advanced species. Any number of animals display "gentleness or fierceness, mildness or cross temper, courage or timidity, fear or confidence, high spirit or low cunning, and, with regard to intelligence, something equivalent to sagacity" (*History of Animals* 588ᵃ 18–21). In some instances, the differences are only quantitative; in other instances, the respective states and capacities are analogous. Human childhood illustrates this principle, for in childhood, human beings present the diminished form of what will flourish after proper and habitual nurturance. Before this occurs, however, the child "hardly differs for the time being from an animal" (*History of Animals* 588ᵇ 1). What man does by intention and design, the lower orders do by instinctual habit.

There are, however, significant differences among all the species —and generally between the genders—in any number of emotional dispositions. These are often heritable, sometimes contingent on circumstances. Animals that are found living tranquilly with each other will cultivate lethal enmities if they subsist on the same food and it becomes scarce (*History of Animals* 608ᵇ 20–25). But eagle and snake, owl and wren, wolf and ass are natural enemies, while the crow and the heron are natural friends. The emotionality in evidence in these circumstances arises from the natural constitution of the animals or from the interaction between this natural constitution and the survival-pressures the animals face. Emotion here is of practical benefit, rendering the creatures more successful in their adaptations and interactions. "In a general way in the lives of animals many resemblances to human life may be observed" (*History of Animals* 612ᵇ 19), whether it is the monogamous bonding of pigeons or the states of war existing between competitors for the same resources.[10]

As Aristotle makes clear in the *Rhetoric*, actions can be brought

---

10. There is a long and informing history of speculation on the extent to which Aristotle's biological treatises are to be regarded as Darwinian or as orthodox evolutionary theory. For an earlier example, consult H. B. Torrey and F. Felin, "Was Aristotle an Evolutionist?" To the extent that Darwinian theory, in its broadest outline, is something of a folk-ethology, informed by animal husbandry, ageless breeding practices, and the like, then of course Aristotle's own naturalistic writings are compatible. But attempts to establish closer parallels are less than convincing.

about by any number and combination of factors: chance, nature, compulsion, habit, reasoning, anger, or appetite (1363ª 5–6). With chance events, the outcomes have no purpose or end and take place rarely and irregularly. Those produced by nature, on the other hand, arise from causes internal to the conditions themselves, the outcomes now being virtually invariant. Acts of compulsion fall beyond the range of the actor's own desires, and those proceeding from habit are, alas, merely habitual; they are performed because they have always been performed. With reasoning, however, actors bring about events for ends that are useful, and do so because of this usefulness. With anger and appetite, the goals of reason may be totally subverted. Actions caused by anger have only revenge as a goal; those caused by appetite, only pleasure.

The "pleasure principle," it should be noted, is not depreciated. All animals seek those conditions that lead to pleasurable or happy states. Aristotle defines such states as, "prosperity combined with excellence . . . independence of life . . . secure enjoyment of the maximum of pleasure . . . a good condition of property and body . . . the power of guarding one's property and body and making use of them. That happiness is one or more of these things, pretty well everybody agrees" (*Rhetoric* 1360ᵇ 4–17). Again, the emphasis is upon what common sense alone makes obvious. Stating the matter most generally, Aristotle identifies the emotions as "all those feelings that so change men as to affect their judgements, and that are also attended by pain or pleasure" (*Rhetoric*, 1378ª 21–22). The emotions are rooted in the appetitional, biological, and entirely natural functions of the animal kingdom. The creature that is rational will come to discover that his judgments are often hostage to this basic biological nature.

It is in the next chapter that virtue and vice are considered, for these turnout to be not a form of emotion but a certain disposition *(hexis)* toward actions that are themselves good or bad. Virtue and vice, then, pertain to matters of principle and thus entail powers of rationality exhibited only by human beings. Emotionality in the domain of principle provides a means of assessing one's character, not merely one's biological states or functions. But at the level at which human nature and animal nature are comparable, the emotions are similar in kind and in effect. They are feelings attended by pain and pleasure, and they impel actions designed to secure pleasure. The pleasure in question, at this basic naturalistic level, is that attained when the *psyche* is in a state of equilibrium or health or sound condition. The emotions excite activity, and this activity—which has pleasure as its end from the perspective of the organism-as-agent—has the soul's own general health in view.

It is the commonsense tone of Aristotle's writings in this area that is the dominant one. He is found, therefore, using such terms as feeling, desire, appetite, and emotion somewhat interchangeably, even confusingly. D. S. Hutchinson, in a careful analysis of the matter, favors the conclusion that Aristotle regards feelings as involving desires for certain objects. He proposes that, "all feelings involve characteristic desires . . . [E]ven in the absence of a general theoretical truth which would establish it, it is reasonable for Aristotle to suppose that all feelings involve distinctive desires, and therefore that a disposition for a certain feeling will also be a disposition for a certain kind of desire."[11]

On this very plausible assumption, Aristotle's theory of motivation and emotion implicitly partitions animals and humans into distinct categories once the conditions that please and pain each genus are acknowledged. To the extent that a person's pleasures and pains are indistinguishable from those that preoccupy animals, the person is less than fully human. And so, when Aristotle states that the virtues are tied up with pleasure and pain, there is already in place a set of assumptions regarding just what should induce these feelings in a virtuous man. These remarks anticipate the topics of the next chapter and are offered here only to round off the purely naturalistic part of Aristotle's systematic Psychology.

Human beings and the advanced species of animals are not radically different in their sensory processes or in the basic principles governing perception, learning, memory, imagination, sleep, dreaming, or even in their overall adjustments to the demands of the environment. Owing to the similarity of biological functions, there are similarities in their states and dispositions and activities. Where the mechanisms are not the same or kindred, they are at least analogous. Human warfare is never impelled by instinct, but at least some combat among animals is triggered by competition and is thus grounded in desires that characterize human communities as well. This is but an example of the comparability of emotional and appetitive forces shaped by environmental pressures and endured equally by man and beast. If there is to be a special science of Man, therefore, it will emerge from such facts of

11. D. S. Hutchinson, *The Virtues of Aristotle*, p. 77.

human life as are not found elsewhere in phylogeny; from desires
of a unique sort and from dispositions toward pain and pleasure
that have no analogues in the infra-human world.

Each species seems to have certain desires in common with
others, but some that are reserved to themselves and that help to
mark off the boundaries within which that species is found. From
everything that can be inferred from their actual behavior, all
animals seem to desire pleasure and safety, conditions favoring
survival and flourishing. Here is that most fundamental analogy in
the domain of desire, the one suggested by the term *eudaimonia*
which, however, is finally applicable solely (and only rarely) to
human life. This is the ultimate *that for the sake of which;* the state
of happiness or flourishing or pleasure that is the goal of behavior.
Clearly, the flourishing state for any given creature is determined
by that creature's faculties. The state of health for a fish requires
an environment that would kill a bird. All sensate creatures seek
pleasure, then, in that all sensate creatures avoid pain and move
toward what is pleasure-producing *for them*. But man is able to
seek the eudaimonic state which is beyond the pleasures of the
senses and is tied to the uniquely rational dimensions of human
life. Many of his actions are impelled by a kind of *pathos* and *orexis*
operative throughout the animal kingdom. But as the human faculties are unique, so also is the human potential for *eudaimonia*,
the life given over to what is most honorable and enduring.[12]

> It is natural, then, that we call neither ox nor horse nor any other
> of the animals happy; for none of them is capable of sharing in
> such activity. For this reason also a boy is not happy; for he is
> not capable of such acts, owing to his age. . . . For there is re-
> quired, as we said, not only complete excellence but also a com-
> plete life. (*Nicomachean Ethics* 1099ᵇ 33–1100ᵃ 5).

With the human *psyche*, then, comes the power of reflection,
choice, deliberation, universalized judgments. With the human
psyche, comes the *the moral point of view* and a nature that is no
longer entirely "natural" in the modern sense.

12. David Furley aptly notices that Aristotle's concept of an object of desire *(orekton)*
goes beyond some external stimulus that has the power of eliciting some emotional or
appetitional response. "[P]eople desire things in the external world," writes Furley, "and
exert themselves to get them, *under certain descriptions,* and their actions cannot be explained without some notion of what each of their goals means *for them*" (emphasis in
original). David J. Furley, "Self-Movers," in Amélie Rorty, ed., *Essays on Aristotle's Ethics,*
p. 63.

SEVEN

Psychology as a Human Science: Rationality, Volition, and the Moral Point of View

Aristotle's Psychology is everywhere a comparative psychology which seeks a scheme of classification that will validly represent the natural order of things. At the end of Book I of *Generation of Animals*, he is found describing nature as an intelligent workman, its creations possessing just those powers and attributes permitting generation and growth. He then observes that it is not only these functions that appear in the animal kingdom. Additionally, all animals acquire knowledge as well, if only because they have the power of sense perception. However, "If we consider the value of this we find that it is of great importance compared with the class of lifeless objects, but of little compared with the use of intellect." (731ᵃ 33–731ᵇ 1)

The essence of a creature is revealed in its *idion ergon*, its particular and identifying work, its vocation or mission. For something to qualify as horse or house, it must possess more than the appearance of a likeness; it must actually do what horses and houses do. Alas, "no hand of bronze or wood . . . can possibly be a hand in more than name. For like a physician in a painting, or like a flute in a sculpture, it will be unable to perform its function" (*Parts of Animals* 640ᵇ 36–641ᵃ 3). A hand has a form and a material composition, but the essential and defining nature of a hand is its function *(eauton ergon)*. The hand incapable of this is either dead or counterfeit. It is a hand in name only. What, then, is *human* nature? It is a nature endowed with an identifying *ergon*, and one established by the very rational powers of the human *psyche*. As a result of rationality, human beings are able to deliberate over means and ends and evaluate these in moral terms. Rationality permits the weighing of options and the choice of those ends that are most fitting for a rational being. It is this choice that establishes the very character of the actor.

Rational thought here is akin to perception in that the actor frames or imagines events for the purpose of judging them to be good or bad. In *On the Soul*, Aristotle provides a concise statement of the process:

> To the thinking soul images serve as if they were contents of perception (and when it asserts or denies them to be good or bad it avoids or pursues them). That is why the soul never thinks without an image. (431ᵃ 15–17)

The choices arising from this process finally record the very character of the actor.[1]

The guidelines by which one is able to discover the better of two or more alternative courses of action are summarized in Book III of the *Topics*. Aristotle at this point offers only an overview, the more

---

1. Aristotle makes this explicit in the *Nicomachean Ethics* at 1111ᵇ 4–6. The interpretation of the relationship between choice *(prohairesis)* and excellence of character *(arete)* offered in the present chapter follows loosely the lines of the argument developed by David Wiggins in "Deliberation and Practical Reason," first published in 1975–76 and reprinted in *Essays on Aristotle's Ethics*, Amélie O. Rorty, ed. That the *idion ergon* is not some specific activity or task but the very *form* of activity is instructively discussed by D. S. Hutchinson, *The Virtues of Aristotle*, especially pp. 60 ff. The quoted passage has itself created confusion and controversy, some of it owing to the accepted translation. In his *Aristotle: De Anima (On the Soul)* Hugh Lawson-Tancred reads 431ᵃ [15–17] thus: "For in the thinking soul, images play the part of precepts, and the assertion or negation of good or bad is invariably accompanied by avoidance or pursuit, which is the reason for the soul's never thinking without an image" (p. 208).

In light of this, he finds it "unclear in any case why Aristotle sees the connection between assertion and negation of good and bad and avoidance and pursuit as the *reason* for the soul's never thinking with(out) an *aisthema*" (p. 248, n. 121). The text states that the thinking or intellectual *psyche (dianoetike)* is possessed of images *(phantasmata)* when thus thinking, in a manner akin to the possession of the objects of perception *(aisthemata)* when *psyche* is actually perceiving something. The claim, then, would seem to entail no more than the proposition that moral judgments are judgments about *something*—various courses of actions, etc.—and this *something* is "pictured" by the thinking soul. Aristotle makes this part of his thesis clear in several places, notably at 432ᵃ [1–15], but is also careful to note that the process of deliberation, though requiring such pictured-content, is not the picture itself (432ᵃ 12–14).

detailed analysis reserved for the major essays in ethics. Moreover, the overview itself pertains only to choices between options that are quite similar and that are not easily ranked by common sense and the consent of the ages. As no one seriously denies that good health or prosperity is desirable, it is not necessary to develop guidelines for choices involving these (*Topics* 116ª 1–5).

Where two courses of action are nearly indistinguishable, it is enough to discover that one of them contains at least one advantage over the other. Aristotle provides a long and occasionally peculiar list of the various advantages one alternative has in relation to another. A less than complete summary is as follows: All other factors being equal, X is more desirable than Y when 1) the benefits of X are more enduring 2) X is known to be preferred by prudent and good persons, 3) X is favored by a proper law, 4) X is the choice of persons with relevant expert knowledge, 5) X is *essentially* better than Y, and not just a better instance of something, 6) X is desired for itself, but Y for something else, 7) X is the cause of what is good and not good by chance or accidentally, 8) X is *absolutely* good, but Y is good only in the particular case, 9) X belongs or is related to that which in itself is superior or more honorable than that to which Y is related, 10) the consequences of X are more productive of good than are the consequences of Y, 11) X carries a greater number of good things with it than does Y, 12) X is more fitting in the given circumstance than is Y, 13) X, even if not good in itself, is more like what is good than Y is, 14) X is more obviously good than Y, or 15) X is harder won than Y (*Topics* 117ª 5–119ª 31).[2]

These items clearly answer to different principles, and each of them requires clarification and qualification. Moreover, just the delineation of such considerations makes evident the need for rationality, since a creature endowed with no more than sense and appetite would be incapable of weighing factors of this sort.

There is another item on the list, however, that deserves special attention. Aristotle is found recommending the superfluous over the necessary, "for the good life is better than mere life, and good life is a superfluity, whereas mere life itself is a necessity" (*Topics* 118ª 6–8). Taken literally, this statement would be more likely to

2. It is clear from the very order in which Aristotle presents these that he is not rank-ordering them on the basis of a scale of worthiness. He seems instead to be delineating what common sense regards as the recommended grounds on which to choose one thing over another.

come from Oscar Wilde than Aristotle! But "the good life," for Aristotle, turns on more subtle considerations.

There is an important distinction to be made between what is *better* and what is *desirable* in life. The former is established only through careful ethical and metaphysical analysis; the latter is a brute fact established by the actual choices recorded by persons in various walks of life. Thus, it is not uncommon for something that is better to be nonetheless undesired:

> There is no necessity that because it is better it should also be more desirable: at least to be a philosopher is better than to make money, but it is not more desirable for a man who lacks the necessities of life. There is superfluity whenever a man possesses the necessities of life and sets to work to secure as well other noble acquisitions. Roughly speaking, perhaps, necessities are more desirable, while superfluities are better. (*Topics* 118ª 8–15)[3]

What is important about this particular distinction is that it acknowledges the contextual determinants of desirability, but not at the price of relativizing the good. It is probably the case that philosophical riches are *better* than money, no matter what anyone might choose, given the option. But it is also the case that a person caught in the grip of poverty and hunger has basic desires that must be answered. Man is at once an animal and a creature cut loose from animality. As was discussed in the previous chapter, his desires are hostage to his animality. It is only when the basic needs of *animal* life have been met that the possibility of a fully *human* life can be exploited. Note, then, that humanity is not something that unfolds or evolves from animality; it is something that transcends it and is often in conflict with it.[4]

This conflicting relationship between animality and humanity warrants additional comment. Aristotle's "human science" is a *characterology*, a theory of "personality" as today's psychologist would call it. What is sought is a classificatory scheme sensitive to the defining attributes of persons, but especially those attributes that explain the conduct of their lives. Put another way, Aristotle's

---

3. This passage is redolent of the conversation between Socrates and aged Cephalus in *Republic* 329–331.

4. There is no "Freudian" theory embedded in Aristotle's psychology. Nor, alas, is there a Darwinian psychology there, even if his ethological treatises are of an evolutionary stripe.

program can be regarded as a "natural history of human types," these types identified according to *character*. The ethical and metaphysical writings are therefore intertwined with Aristotle's psychological discourses. What sort of person Smith is cannot be decided until there is in place a moral science by which to assess Smith's character. But then the requirements of morality cannot be deduced in a psychological vacuum. Moral concepts (e.g., obligation, blame, duty, praise, right and wrong) must be grounded in assumptions as to what falls within the reach of human potentialities and attributes. The naturalistic treatises have carefully established the animalistic side of Smith. Little of this, however, informs Aristotle's distinctively *human* psychology, for the latter arises from psychic faculties *(dunameis)* and dispositions *(hexeis)* unique to human beings. If, however, as shown in the previous chapter, a human being is so situated as to be controlled by animalistic desires and needs, there will be very little of the generically *human* attributes in evidence. The affairs of the body will mask the dispositions of the soul. (Here, then, is an echo of Plato's *desmoterion* theory of the relationship between body and soul). In the circumstance, it is not possible to discern what sort of *person* Smith is, because personhood itself has been suspended. To know what sort of person Smith is, it becomes necessary to observe Smith's choice of actions when it is in his power to do what is noble. At this point, the often debated distinction between what a given person requires to be happy and those things that are good *for* man *qua* man becomes a distinction without a principled difference. What any man must finally choose if he would attain *eudaimonia*, as will be discussed further, are just those forms of activity that answer to what is good for man *qua* man; forms of activity regulated by reason and conforming to the standards of excellence.[5]

Returning now to the contracted list of the grounds on which to rest preferred courses of action, it can be seen that Aristotle invokes a number of conceptually different criteria. There are grounds for choosing X over Y that are entirely *conventional;* grounds that are essentially *logical;* grounds that are merely *technical;* grounds that

5. This point is discussed in several places by Aristotle, but most directly in the *Eudemian Ethics* 1228ª 2–7. On the debate regarding what man requires for happiness versus what is good *for* man, D. S. Hutchinson concludes: "The life according to excellence is the best life for me, but not from the point of view of my interests especially, or even of morality, or indeed from any point of view at all. It simply is the best life for me, for it is the best life that a creature like me can live, and it is the life that all normal, natural, and perfect people do in fact lead" (*The Virtues of Aristotle*, p. 68).

are utterly *consequentialist;* grounds that are irreducibly *moral.* It may be the case that the best reason for choosing X is just that most doctors recommend it, and what is sought is a medical remedy. It may be the case that there is no good reason for choosing X over Y, except that most people have chosen it and still do choose it. At a commonsense level, it is reasonable to assume that, if there is no more compelling ground for choice, conventional wisdom or the judgment of experts is sufficient. There are, however, things that are good in themselves, that are more honorable and noble, quite apart either from the conventional wisdom or from what others might think about them or from the usefulness of the consequences. A good man is one who chooses these things and who is made happy by choosing them.

The question that immediately arises, of course, is how one is to identify those actions that are more honorable and good in themselves. More tellingly, how is one to locate the *right* course of action and be committed to it apart from considerations of utility? Here is a fundamental moral question, a question of ethical theory which Aristotle typically (if not always explicitly) approaches as a psychologist.[6] The Socratics ask in *Meno* and in *Protagoras* whether virtue can be taught. Aristotle, too, now must weigh the question.

It is a question laced with subtle problems and deep implications, even ignoring the transparent difficulty of establishing the nature of virtue itself. In the *Nicomachean Ethics* (1151[a] 12–19), Aristotle seems to argue that a virtuous man cannot be produced by reason, but only by nature and by conditioning.[7] If this were all he had to say, the entire body of his ethical writings would become trivial. From the mere fact that some condition arises as a result of "nature," nothing justificatory follows. It is as much within the province of vice as of virtue to claim the sanctions of "nature." As Aristotle himself pointedly remarks, "it is absurd to make external circumstances responsible, and not oneself, as being caught by such [tempting] attractions, and to make oneself responsible for

6. As T. H. Irwin has noted, Aristotle's ethical theory "is based on his psychology and therefore on his metaphysics; the starting point of ethics is a feature of human agents which is a part of their soul and essence" (p. 50). T. H. Irwin, "The Metaphysical and Psychological Basis of Aristotle's Ethics," in Rorty, ed., *Essays on Aristotle's Ethics.*

7. This has led some to despair of finding an adequate theory of morality at all in Aristotle's philosophy. Richard Robinson, for example, concludes that "If we adopt the method of Aristotle we never progress at all, so that, unless we have had the extraordinary luck to be established right on the end by our teachers, we shall never get any nearer to it" (p. 91). Richard Robinson, "Aristotle on Akrasia," in J. Barnes, M. Schofield, and R. Sorabji, eds., *Articles on Aristotle*, vol. 2.

noble acts but the pleasant objects responsible for base acts" (*Nicomachean Ethics* 1010^b 13–15). Similarly, those actions that do no more than reflect the regulative effects of conditioning or habituation find their principle external to the actors and therefore leave them neither praiseworthy nor blameworthy.

But a tangled web of difficulties awaits one who would develop a theory that identifies both the actions that qualify as good and the sort of agent (character) from whom such actions proceed. An action so called may have more than one outcome, thus leaving in doubt what its actual end was. Oedipus intends to kill not his father but a man in the road whose name happens to be Laius— who is his father. Of course, Oedipus does not know this, but the fact illustrates a general problem, viz., the extent to which an actor must actually be informed as to the full effects of an action in order to be said to have acted with intent. If the condition of intentionality requires complete and infallible knowledge, then no action will ever be intentional. Then, too, since actions have happiness as their end, it makes no sense to say that virtuous actions are done for their own sake; they are done for the sake of *eudaimonia*. Is there more than one *telos?* Moreover, the roster of those principles governing choice leaves the entire matter unsettled, for it takes any number of ends—health, prosperity, happiness—as ends in themselves, meaning there is finally nothing final!

These are difficult problems, and any number of commentators have suggested that there is a manifest incoherence in Aristotle's overall theory which seeks to tie together both his psychological and his ethical principles. The latter principles spring from the former, and close attention to his psychological assumptions reveals his ethical writings to be not only coherent but perhaps superior to alternative formulations. It is important to discover the connecting arguments that merge the ethical and the psychological into a coherent framework.

As has been discussed, Aristotle's Psychology is developmental and characterological. The concept of *eudaimonia* answers to this description. No one is born with a developed sense of virtue, nor is the infant able to plan a course of action for a lifetime. Early in the course of development, when passion and appetite still rule, behavior is hedonistic and utilitarian. No one, says Aristotle, would choose to return to this tormented stage of life (*Eudemian Ethics* 1215^b 22–24). This does not mean that appetites are entirely cut off from reason in a creature otherwise rationally endowed. As Aristotle

97

notes in the *Rhetoric*, there are in addition to the natural appetites of hunger and thirst the *rational appetites* "which we are induced to have; there are many things we desire to see or get because we have been told of them and induced to believe them good" (1370^a 25–27). These appetites are prevalent within the human community where learning by deliberate instruction is possible. Children can come to be moved by cravings of one sort or another, but without reliance on such *natural* appetites as hunger and thirst. Clearly, therefore, instruction can create human desires distinct from those that arise naturally as a function of the states of the body. But at the beginning of the same section, Aristotle reminds his auditors that pleasure generically is "a movement by which the soul as a whole is consciously brought into its normal state of being. . . . It must therefore be pleasant for the most part to move towards a natural state of being" (*Rhetoric* 1369^b 34–1370^a 4). A process of habituation or conditioning can lead to the right sort of action becoming, as it were, "second nature" and therefore pleasurable (because entirely natural) when performed. If it is possible to uncover that state of being that is, indeed, natural for the soul, then it follows that pleasure will ensue when activity produces or promotes that state; or, better, the pleasure just *is* the activity of establishing such a state. Children cannot be expected either to know what is natural for the soul or to achieve it. Hence, the conditioning of appropriate behavior precedes an awareness of those higher principles which the behavior itself instantiates. Practice makes perfect now in yet another sense!

Reservations regarding rationality are not to be construed as a sign of flagging rationalism on Aristotle's part. Rather, he is soberly and well aware of the incomplete rationality of children and of the consequence of this: They cannot find moral imperatives in rational arguments. What they possess by nature is the potentiality for this discovery, but the principle itself arises cognitively out of the habitual behaviors installed by the community of adults. The principles are instilled only by the behavior that is installed. This is the central point. If the child is ever to develop in such a way as to supply the practical syllogism with content, the content must come from what is already a broad and rich range of behavioral options that have met with various consequences. Where early life has been given over entirely to the passions of the moment and to noncontingent pleasures, the person may come to be beyond rehabilitation. It is, after all, the history of activity itself that supplies

the possibilities for rationality, including the possibility of ordering one's actions rationally. There is, then, no contradiction and
no incoherence in that part of Aristotle's program which at once
subscribes to a rationalistic theory of morals and at the same
time insists that man is not *made* virtuous by rational argument.

Turning to the proposition that Aristotle's thesis includes (inco-
herently) too many *teloi*, the complaint seems to rest on a confusion
as to the real nature of *eudaimonia*, and even some confusion as to
what is meant by a *telos*. The state of *eudaimonia* is not one of
ephemeral delights or even one that is describable chiefly in sensory terms. As David Wiggins has said,

> Unlike utility, eudaimonia is not built up from a set of packages
> of goods . . . which the theory claims the agent will seek to maxi-
> mize if he is rational. . . . The judgment that one course of action
> is better than another is not arrived at in this way at all, but by
> reference to the agent's pre-existing conception (constantly in-
> formed and reshaped by circumstance) of the life that it is good
> for a man to attempt to realize.[8]

Eudamonia is, then, not some mysterious condition of being that
one somehow falls into as a result of good genes or sound instruction; it is an actually *conceived* state of being, toward which a
person strives. A life becomes a work of art evolving, the artist
altering the methods, the materials, and even the conception of the
intended work as he goes along. Though constructive behavior is
initially conditioned, the child moves beyond the stage of animality
and into the stage of rationality. In this stage and state—and
equipped with behavioral dispositions that have been anchored
to creature comforts—this now rational being can finally come
to order his conduct and plan his life in an *authentic* manner;
i.e., the conduct now reflects what the actor himself has chosen
for himself, cognizant not only of alternatives, but of the fact
that such choices in the past were shaped by forces external to himself.

That "end" toward which the agent's actions aim is, moreover,
not sharply cut off from the actions themselves. Anthony Kenny offers an instructive reading of *ta pros to telos*, urging that it is better

8. David Wiggins, "Weakness of the Will," in Rorty, ed., *Essays on Aristotle's Ethics*, p.
261.

rendered as *ways and means,* "since many of Aristotle's 'means' to
happiness are in fact ways of being happy."[9] This is not to say that
some means to a desired end are not themselves undesirable; e.g.,
denying oneself a current pleasure in the interest of a longer-term
good; or engaging in tiring exercise for the purpose of promoting
good health. Rather, it is to recognize that ongoing virtuous actions
are at once a source of, an expression of, and a means to, pleasure.

Aristotle does not have too many *teloi* to contend with, each one
violating the claimed finality of the rest. It is not the case that his
system lacks an identifiable and single *that* in the *that for the sake
of which.* Confusion on this point—which seems not to be Aristotle's—is occasioned by regarding *eudaimonia* as some sort of
"super pleasure," on the same continuum with cold drinks on a hot
day or a warm bath after a day's labor. What distinguishes these
from *eudaimonia* is that the latter is not an episodic detail to be
added to or subtracted from life; *it is the very form of life.* Although
good health is, in one sense, an end in itself, it is not sought without
qualification. One can be, after all, in excellent health but otherwise miserable. J. L. Ackrill states and then removes the paradox
this way:

> A is more final than B if though B is sought for its own sake (and
> hence is indeed a final and not merely intermediate goal) it is
> also sought for the sake of A. And that end is more final than any
> other, final without qualification *(teleion aplos),* which is always
> sought for its own sake and never for the sake of anything else.
> Such, [Aristotle] continues, is *eudaimonia.*[10]

There are ends that are constitutive of *eudaimonia* and are sought
for themselves because they are inextricably tied up with *eudaimonia.* The latter, recognized as *the most desirable* form of life,
carries with it any number of conditions of the body and of the
mind. These conditions are sought for their own sake not in competition with *eudaimonia,* but as its complements. What Aristotle

9. Anthony Kenny, *Aristotle's Theory of the Will,* p. 149. It is on pp. 164–166 that
Professor Kenny answers most economically those who have found missing in Aristotle's
psychology a theory of the will. In this same estimable work, he provides convincing
arguments for the conclusion that many, if not most, of the problematic features of Aristotle's ethical works are illusory; they arise from the failure of commentators to distinguish
between Aristotle's own theses and those of others which he presents by way of historical
summary.
10. J. L. Akrill, "Aristotle on *Eudaimonia*" in Rorty, ed., *Essays on Aristotle's Ethics,* p.
21.

advocates, then, is a life in which all that should matter to anyone flourishes. But, as D. S. Hutchinson observes,

> Aristotle avoids the low road of justification and avoids the diffi-
> cult task which Plato set himself, to show that the life of virtue
> will appeal to every man who thinks clearly about it and that the
> life of vice will be unwelcome to every man who thinks clearly
> about it, propositions which are, after all, false.[11]

Aristotle is a realist, not an idealist regarding human nature. He knows that clear thinking, if it is not *correct* thinking, will pardon vice as easily at it will applaud virtue. *Eudaimonia* is not for everyone.

Throughout his ethical writings, Aristotle focuses on actions that are voluntary *(hekousios)* and that arise from a deliberated choice *(prohairesis)*. In the *Nicomachean Ethics*, Book III begins with ac-knowledgment that both legislators and those concerned with ex-cellence of character *(arete)* must be able to distinguish between the voluntary and the involuntary *(akousios)*.[12] The distinction is not always easy to make, however. An action performed under duress, for example, is compelled, but is not for this reason so obviously *akousios*. The example he offers is the decision to jet-tison cargo during a storm at sea (1110ᵃ 8–11). The captain does not want to destroy the cargo, but, in the circumstance, is left with no choice. The point is that, in the circumstance, he does *choose*.

> Such actions, then, are mixed, but are more like voluntary ac-
> tions; for they are worthy of choice at the time when they are
> done, and the end of an action is relative to the occasion. Both
> the terms, then, "voluntary" and "involuntary", must be used
> with reference to the moment of action. (1110ᵃ 11–14).

This and the sentences just following it are central to Aristotle's theory of *volition* and may be offered as at least a partial reply to those who deny he even had a concept of "will" of the modern sort. A violent storm creates an occasion which threatens the lives of the crew. A valuable cargo is in the hold, and it is the mission of the

11. D. S. Hutchinson, *The Virtues of Aristotle*, p. 71.
12. The word *arete* is often translated as "excellence," though the fit between the Greek and various English nouns is not smooth. *Moral excellence* is the subject of the *Nicomachean Ethics*, and in this context "good character" or "excellence of character" conveys the meaning of *arete*.

crew to deliver it to its intended destination. Of course, "in the abstract . . . no one would choose any such act in itself" (1110ᵃ 18–19) as throwing the cargo overboard. Thus, being forced to do so is being compelled to do something that would *in the abstract* be *akousios*. But the captain and crew are not deliberating in the abstract. Rather, they face the real dilemma of losing the ship—including the cargo and their own lives—or jettisoning the cargo in the hope of saving everything but the cargo itself. It is *at the moment* of the action that they may be said to act voluntarily.

What Aristotle rejects here is the thesis that actions under duress are invariably *determined* in the way that the behavior of inanimate objects is determined. The fact that a force *(bia)* has been brought to bear on an actor in such a way as to deny others the right to call the action utterly unforced *(abiastos)*, does not mean the action is involuntary. Rather, actions are totally compelled only, "when the cause is in the external circumstances and the agent contributes nothing" (1110ᵇ 2–3).

And this clarifies at least one of the grounds on which Aristotle would have to reject the Socratic doctrine according to which the summons of virtue is irresistible to the reasonable man. If, indeed, "someone were to say that pleasant and noble objects have a compelling power, forcing us from without, all acts for him would be compulsory" (1110ᵇ 9–10), and thus beyond the ambit of praise or blame. A rational being has the intellectual power to take a skeptical stance in regarding any and every moral claim, at least for purposes of argument. The summons of virtue is finally a species of *logical* necessity once the rational arguments have been developed, but not a species of the "irresistible" or of anything grounded in appetite.

It is also in Book III of the *Nicomachean Ethics* that Aristotle wrestles with the Socratic thesis that would regard actions performed in ignorance as being involuntary.[13] In examining the thesis, he finds it important to differentiate those actions that are not voluntary into the categories of the involuntary *(akousios)* and the nonvoluntary *(ouch ekousios)*. The distinction then permits him to claim that all actions committed in ignorance are *nonvoluntary*,

---

13. The version of the thesis in the dialogues is stated most clearly but then quickly qualified in the *Laws*, Book IX, 860–862. Here the Athenian Stranger informs Cleinias and Megillus that "the unjust man may be bad, but . . . is bad against his will," and that it would be contradictory to argue that "an action which is voluntary should be done involuntarily" (Jowett translation).

but that only those producing pain and regret may be said to be *involuntary* (1110^b 17–18). The claim arises from a distinction between cognitive and affective contributions to actions. A person who, in the relevant cognitive respects, is ignorant of each and every possible consequence of an action now being performed cannot be said to act with volition. To act with volition is to act *for the sake of* some real, perceived, imagined, or possible end. To be totally ignorant of the latter is just to be in a nonvolitional state. Volition simply doesn't enter into any correct explanation of the behavior.

Where the consequences of an action are, however, painful, or where they produce regret, it is clear that the action was compelled. No one freely chooses to cause himself pain. No one freely chooses a course of action known to warrant regret. As in the instance of the ship in a turbulent sea, there are gray areas where it is not at all clear whether the action should be regarded as voluntary or involuntary. Even in the case of the storm-tossed crew, however, the jettisoning of the cargo was *nonvoluntary*, though in one sense it was *involuntary*. Rather, it was required by the circumstances and thus turned out to be the only *choice* left to captain and crew.

The deliberated choice *(prohairesis)* is something that is voluntary, "but not the same thing as the voluntary; the latter extends more widely. For both children and the other animals share in voluntary action, but not in choice, and acts done on the spur of the moment we describe as voluntary, but not as chosen" *(Nicomachean Ethics* 1111^b 7–10). In the same place, Aristotle goes on to say that animals have appetites and emotions, and yet do not have choice, and the incontinent man *(akrates)* acts in response to his appetites but not through choice. Nor is choice a species of opinion, for the latter does not peg someone as a particular kind of person, whereas one's choices do reflect one's basic character. Neither is a choice a wish, for wishes can have the impossible as their object, though choices cannot.

Aristotle's reflections on the nature of choice bring him to the conclusion that an action that is truly *chosen* is one that is initiated only when an end or goal is itself chosen. What is done out of passion or appetite or the impulses of the moment is unchosen specifically in the sense that the consequences of the action were not the productions of rational deliberation. What is done under such conditions may be regarded as voluntary but not as chosen. It is clear now why Aristotle insists often that one's basic character is revealed through *prohairesis*. What a person after due deliberation and with all of the qualifying apparatus of reason finally comes to want proclaims the sort of person he is. Once this goal is set, the only room left for deliberation is the means to it.

In an often misunderstood passage, Aristotle concludes that, "We deliberate not about ends but about what contributes to ends. . . . Having set the end [we] consider how and by what means it is to be attained" (1112^b 12–16). Far from making a moral point to the effect that the end justifies the means, Aristotle here offers only the truism that, once a goal is fixed, what remains to be considered is the method of attaining it.

Any goal worth consideration in this context is, as Richard Sorabji has stated, "not merely . . . particular goals but . . . the good life in general . . . with a view to the best." [14] Again, goals answering to this qualification mark out a person as having a defining character, for goals of this sort specify the life that person would elect for himself were no more than his own choice required. The correct choices here require a special form of wisdom, *practical wisdom (phronesis)*, which functions in the ethical domain the way *praktikos* functions in the realm of utility. If it is the person's character that is under consideration, then the choices must be his authentically. His actions (and his character) are, therefore, *good* only if he has intentionally aimed at the good because of a developed *hexis* toward the good.[15] It is contradictory to declare an action good when it has proceeded from malign motives, even if the consequences are desirable. So too is it inapt to praise someone who just accidentally caused something desirable to happen. An action is in itself good—and the actor is himself good—when what is done is done *in order that the good prevail*. The disposition of the actor is determinative, and this is why his character is to be assessed according to his *hexeis*, not his feelings or appetites.

Before considering the particular types of "personality" that Aristotle's Psychology subsumes, it is important to emphasize the central place given to *self-determination* in the ethical treatises. Early instruction and example are important, and a species-wide

14. Richard Sorabji, "Aristotle on the Role of Intellect in Virtue," in Rorty ed., *Essays on Aristotle's Ethics*, p. 295.
15. Sir David Ross has expressed the relationship this way: "Aristotle here lays his finger with precision on the distinction between the two elements involved in a completely good action—(a) that the thing done should be the right thing to do in the circumstances, and (b) that it should be done from a good motive" (*Aristotle*, p. 194).

tendency toward the good is granted in these treatises. But in the end, the adult rational human being is regarded as being responsible for what he is and for what he now is in the process of becoming. If there is to be exculpation for a defective character, it is only by establishing that the causal factors were entirely outside the actor's self and beyond the actor's control. It is not enough to show that one simply has odd opinions or eccentric tastes, or that the innocent habits of a lifetime have now rendered one less than able to strive for honor.

> Now some one may say that all men aim at the apparent good, but have no control over how things appear to him; but the end appears to each man in a form answering to his character. We reply that if each man is somehow responsible for the state he is in, he will also be somehow responsible for how things appear ... for we are ourselves somehow part-causes of our states of character, and it is by being persons of a certain kind that we assume the end to be so and so. (*Nicomachean Ethics* 1113ª 32–1114ᵇ 25)

What Aristotle rejects is a psychological determinism that reduces choice to the diminished and counterfeit options afforded by socialization, or an even more radical determinism that absorbs rationality and morality into the physical sciences. He recognizes the force of that theory of "constitutive luck" which would offer hereditary explanations of eudaimonic and non-eudaimonic pursuits (1114ª 32–1114ᵇ 16). But the radical versions of such a theory not only pardon the evil man but also deny the possibility of a praiseworthy man. If nature is the cause of ignorance of what is truly noble, it must also be the cause of a recognition of what is truly noble and, in each case, the person *per se* takes no part. This, however, is simply false, for there are clearly actions that are fully chosen, and this means that choice is possible. Thus, even if some naturally produced defect prevented one from comprehending noble ends, specific evil actions remain blameworthy. "In the case of the bad man there is equally present that which depends on himself in his actions even if not in his end" (1114ᵇ 20–21).

Aristotle's human Psychology is in the main voluntaristic therefore, which is to say that it is compatible with his ethical and political theories. It is a *self-actualizing* Psychology, though more rigorous and reasoned than the latter-day "humanistic" versions. Moreover, it is a stage- and state-Psychology in that there is an undefined period in life, after childhood, wherein the ripened rational powers of the person permit him to take charge of the significant parts of his life. But the rule of reason is "royal," not tyrannical. One may disobey and follow instead the demands of emotion and appetite. Reason, emotion, and appetite all make strong claims on the actor, and his character is revealed in the dispositions he has toward each.[16]

What reason dictates is a course of action that brings the soul toward a natural state, a state of flourishing and of excellence. Clearly, this is not a state easily reached or easily maintained. More common are those states that fall short or swing wildly past it, and this for several reasons. Persons may grossly misperceive the situations in which they find themselves. They may be ignorant of the actual consequences awaiting their intended actions. They may be so moved by the pressures of the moment as not to give rationality its due. All of these factors may operate on those who, nonetheless, have the same objectives. In the face of a threat, one of three dispositions may prove to be dominant. The disposition toward self-interest may be so overpowering that the threat leads to paralyzing fear or unprincipled retreat. In this instance, the actor displays the vice of cowardice. Another person, so utterly disposed toward confidence, underestimates the threat and thus behaves rashly, his actions being the counterfeit of courage. The man of courage, however, correctly assesses the danger and thus is fearful, but also is disposed to do his duty and thus takes the proper course of action. The virtue or excellence of courage is that disposition that is equidistant between the vicious poles of excess and deficiency. Courage, then, "is a mean with regard to fear and confidence' (1115ᵃ 7). It is praiseworthy, whereas heedlessness is not. The man faced with such a danger but who knows no fear whatever is simply a madman to whom no honor is due (1115ᵇ 24–30). As with courage, so with all the virtues the criteria are the same: The actor is virtuous when the act is performed in behalf of a noble end, when the end itself is identified through rational deliberation, and when it proceeds from a principle within the actor.

16. Discussing the matter of personal responsibility, T. H. Irwin concludes that "All that Aristotle says and implies . . . is perfectly compatible with his being a determinist". The argument Professor Irwin develops is one in which all of the factors that finally establish a given character are causally determinative as regards the actor's actual choices. Some of the factors, properly understood, are self-determined, however, and so the voluntarisitic aspect of Aristotle's theory remains undiminished. T. H. Irwin, "Reason and Responsibility in Aristotle," in Rorty, ed., *Essays on Aristotle's Ethics*, p. 142.

106

A more complete picture of the theory is afforded by the example of anger or of the passions in general. Suppose Smith has been deeply offended in an altercation with several other men, all of them armed and ruthless. In a nearly reflexive response to the offense, Smith attacks his tormentors, disregarding their numbers and their arms. Has he been courageous, and is his action therefore virtuous?

> Men . . . as well as beasts, suffer pain when they are angry, and are pleased when they exact their revenge; those who fight for these reasons, however, are pugnacious but not brave; for they do not act for the sake of the noble nor as reason directs, but from feeling; they have, however, something akin to courage. (*Nicomachean Ethics* 1117ᵃ 6–9)

What they have that is akin to courage is the disposition to act in defiance of fear. What they lack is governance by a noble principle. The theory of virtue is, nevertheless, a theory of actions and dispositions to act, not a "cognitive" theory concerned to solve abstract moral problems. A person of noble character is not arrested by Hamlet's introspections, but neither is he impelled by Lear's dementia. Where there is in the developed character the virtue of courage, the period of rational deliberation has long since become history and the actor is now ready to respond without delay. Acts that are foreseen may be chosen by calculation," says Aristotle, whereas "sudden actions [are] in accordance with one's state of character" (1117ᵃ 20–21). There is no contradiction here. Virtue is not reason by another name, though it exists only in rational creatures. Excellence of character—*virtue*—is the overriding state or disposition[17] to act according to principles authorized by reason and preponderant over the passions. In its full development, excellence of character just is the person's *nature*.

A consideration of the vices makes clearer Aristotle's theory of virtue. In each instance, there is an emotional or affective component, but one grounded in a principle or judgment. Together, these cognitive and affective events both shape and proceed from a disposition. The given affective *state (diathesis)* can, by prolonged indulgence, become an abiding disposition *(hexis)*. Consider the difference between envy *(phthonos)* and emulation *(zelos)*. Both are

---

17. Aristotle distinguishes between a disposition *(hexis)* and a state *(diathesis)* on the basis of the enduring nature of the former *(Categories* 8ᵇ 27–28). The English word *disposition* has been used almost exclusively in this chapter wherever "state" might be confusing.

aroused by the good fortune and standing of those with whom one would be inclined to identify himself; those of similar age and class. In both instances, it is what is judged to be good that is perceived and that triggers a desire. But the envious person in this case is disposed to resent the excellence of another and to wish that it were not so; whereas the virtuous man will strive to emulate this excellence and thus increase it (*Rhetoric* 1387ᵇ 21–1388ᵇ 29). The characters of one who envies and one who emulates goodness are different. In one case there is the desire to limit or remove what is good, in the other the desire to increase it.

But here is still another point at which the issue of so-called "weakness of the will" *(akrasia)* would appear to be an embarrassment to the theory. The problem in summary is this: If an actor performs X intentionally, then the actor was disposed to perform X. To have a disposition to perform X and at the same time to be able to perform X is, alas, to be able to *choose* X over any and every non-X action. Smith is now discovered to have gambled away the family fortune, and offers in his own defense that he is a "compulsive gambler" whose behavior is to be explained as arising from the weakness of his will.[18] Richard Robinson has summarized the four solutions to the problem offered in the *Nicomachean Ethics*.[19] The actor may in general have knowledge of the right course of action but not be contemplating it at the specific time at which the (acratic) action is taken. Secondly, consequential actions typically reflect the conclusions generated by the "practical syllogism" but, although the actor may possess the universal (major) premise, he may not apply it correctly in the given circumstance. Or the person may be temporarily incapacitated (by sleep, by disease, by alcohol) and, although at other times he *knows* the ruling principle, he does not *now* employ it. In all three of these qualifying conditions, the focus is on what the actor knows *at the time of the action.* As noted earlier in connection with the jettisoning of cargo, it typically is at the moment of commitment that the volitional properties of the action must be assessed. Accordingly, ignorance or forgetfulness or distraction at *that* moment can prevent an actor from conforming his conduct to the dictates of principle. The fourth solution is one

18. This issue has received frequent attention. Several of the more informing works are Donald Davidson, "How Is Weakness of the Will Possible?" in Joel Feinberg, ed., *Moral Concepts;* Richard Robinson, "Aristotle on Akrasia," ch. 8 in Barnes, Schofield, and Sorabji, eds., *Articles on Aristotle,* vol. 2; David Wiggins, "Weakness of the Will Commensurability, and the Objects of Deliberation and Desire," ch. 14 in Rorty, ed., *Essays on Aristotle's Ethics.*

19. Richard Robinson, "Aristotle on Akrasia," p. 80 ff.

in which there is at once a conflict between major premises (e.g., "All sweets are appealing" and "Do not indulge your senses to excess"), but the acratic—moved by desire—neglects the second prescription.

Commentators critical of Aristotle's efforts to explain intemperance have correctly noted the failure of his arguments as formal proofs, but seem to expect such proofs because of the formal nature of the "practical syllogism" itself. Aristotle, however, develops not only logical but *psychological* explanations for intemperance. One who fails to follow the dictates of reason and who pursues instead the path to quick gratification is a culpable person. His will is weak *because he has weakened it,* and he has weakened it by holding it to too low a standard of justification. In other words, the acratic has installed (if only for the moment) the wrong universal premise or has supplied the wrong particulars into the arguments of the practical syllogism. John Locke remarked that madmen reason rightly from wrong premises, and Aristotle would extend the thesis to cover vice as well.

None of this is to be taken as indicating that Aristotle's theory of vice is reducible to an ignorance-theory of the sort defended by Socrates. There is all the difference between a willful suspension of reason and a medical mishap that strips one of reason; all the difference between vague and fleeting perceptions resulting from unfavorable conditions, and self-imposed blindnesses arising from a desire not to face the facts; all the difference between acting wrongly because of a pardonably incorrect belief, and subscribing to a dubious belief as a way of rationalizing evil actions. It is in these respects that the actor can be held responsible for his vices. And yet, what survives even these distinctions is that older Socratic theory that refuses to make knowledge *(episteme)* a slave to passion or appetite. What the acratic does is first corrupt his knowledge, and then act in a manner that would be permissible were the facts as he has made them out to be. (People can make their own thirsts, after all) (1154^b 3–4). He has replaced as the focus and end of his actions that state of *eudaimonia* that reason might secure with things that are less abiding. Following David Wiggins, it may be said that the acratic has made substitutions for what reason shows to be simply *incommensurable.*[20]

How is weakness of the will possible?

20. David Wiggins, "Weakness of the Will."

> Nor can the same man have practical wisdom and be inconti-
> nent; for it has been shown that a man is at the same time
> practically wise, and good in respect of character. Further, a
> man has practical wisdom not by knowing only but by acting;
> but the incontinent man is unable to act. (*Nicomachean Ethics*
> 1152ª 7–9)

Weakness of the will is not finally an intellectual condition in
which *episteme* has been enslaved by various *orexeis*. It is the *behavioral* state in which moral stamina has become diminished through
disuse. The conduct displayed by such persons does not become
pardonable or acceptable on relativistic grounds or on a showing
that most persons are comparably weak or distracted. What pleases
the vicious, says Aristotle, is like what might please the sick or
infirm, or what appearances are to those with defective vision
(1173ᵇ 21–26). There is a test that pleasure itself must pass. What
the various pleasures are bound up with are *activities*, and those
pleasures are good or bad to the extent that they are grounded in
activities which are themselves good or bad. "For to each activity
there is a proper pleasure" (1175ᵇ 26). And pleasure itself is specific
to each kind of creature depending on its nature and its *erga*.
Accordingly, "[T]hat which is proper to each thing is by nature
best and most pleasant for each thing; for man, therefore, the life
according to intellect is best and pleasantest, since intellect more
than anything else *is* man. This life therefore is also the happiest"
(*Nicomachean Ethics* 1178ª 5–8).

The character that is formed by and throughout life is an organic
product of one's capacities, one's experiences, the activities that
have become habitual. In youth, passions are strong and are grati-
fied in an unprincipled way, these states at once expressing the
conditions of youth itself, the incomplete socialization of the passions, and certain biological attributes that are strongest in youth
(*Rhetoric* 1389ª). What is excessive in youth tends to be deficient in
old age (*Rhetoric* 1389ᵇ 13–1390ª 23). It is only in the *prime of life*
that these tendencies are balanced and centered on the mean.

> To put it generally, all the valuable qualities that youth and age
> divide between them are united in the prime of life, while all
> their excesses or defects are replaced by moderation and fitness.
> The body is in its prime from thirty to thirty-five; the mind about
> forty-nine. (*Rhetoric* 1390ᵇ 6–10)

To look for deductive certainties in Aristotle's moral Psychology is to fail to see this Psychology as one that is beholden to Aristotle's natural science, but a natural science in which the unique capacities of *human* nature must be explained. It is to fail to recognize that the flourishing life, *eudaimonia,* is not the conclusion of a formal argument but something that is possible for a rational being and known perhaps only by the one who is living it.

The attainment of such a life is not guaranteed, to say the least, and faces high hurdles at every turn. To live a virtuous life is not easy at the outset. The individual person who might hope to attain *eudiamonia* will need direction, care, and good examples, all of this coming from the society and the culture that surrounds him. *Polis andra didaska.* Man is taught by the city, and the goals of Aristotle's *human* science must therefore be realized by a *social* science.

EIGHT

Psychology as a Social Science: The Self and the Social Order

A *eudaimonic* life is the life lived by a certain kind of person. Aristotle begins his *Eudemian Ethics* with an examination of the sources of such a life. Does *eudaimonia* come about by nature? Is it inherited, the way height and complexion seem to be? Is one chosen for it by the gods and thereupon raised to so lofty a level of existence? Is it reached through courses or a study of how-to books? Is it acquired by training or is one finally just lucky? Clearly, a person can achieve some kind of happiness as a result of any one or any combination of such factors, but it remains to be established just what must be created within a person such that *eudiamonia* is the resulting life.

The candidates (*Eudemian Ethics* 1214ᵃ 33–35) served up by traditional thinking and by common sense, are Wisdom *(phronesis)*, Virtue or Excellence of Character *(arete)*, and Pleasure *(edone)*. The person who would liberate himself from the clutches of the older theories, however, and actually undertake the serious business of life, must set a clear goal before himself and pursue it.[1] If, as is

1. The choice of *edone* makes clear that Aristotle is speaking chiefly of sensual pleasures, such as those answering to the Latin *voluptas*. He is, then, speaking of *eudaimonia* as *hedonism*. Werner Jaeger described Aristotle's emphasis on the practical within the context

unarguable, *eudaimonia* is the goal, then it is necessary to discover its nature and the conditions that are indispensable to achieving it. The lives that go along with the three major candidates are the philosophical (the gift of *phronesis*), the political (which depends upon *arete*), and the hedonistic (via *edone*). The first of these would seek *eudaimonia* through a life befitting the philosopher *(philosophos);* the second, through the careers of citizen and statesman *(politikos);* the third, in the preoccupations of the voluptuary *(apolaustikos).*

The pursuit itself, as noted in the preceding chapter, calls for that sharpened focus by which the "golden mean" is kept in view, lest the excesses and deficiencies of vice put one on the wrong track. It is at 1220^b 39–1221^a 12 in his *Eudemian Ethics* that Aristotle actually summarizes the vices and virtues in tabular form (see table 1).

Now, the most obvious characteristic of these forty-two attributes is that nearly every one of them either entails or requires or derives its very meaning from a *social* context. The attributes are personal, but they form just that *persona* that alerts the community to the sort of person one is. In short, the Table of Virtues—though tied to that most intimate aspect of life, the very *self*—is also a table of social graces, social duties, and social expectations. It is with the management of these that moral excellence *(arete)* must be occupied, and it is through the lifelong cultivation of habits that "these faculties belong to us either in a reasonable way or the opposite" (1220^a 18–19).

In both *Nicomachean Ethics* (1179^a 35–1179^b 31) and *Eudemian Ethics* (1216^b 21–25), Aristotle recognizes the importance of a knowledge of what constitutes moral excellence, but he also knows that the whole point of such knowledge is to permit one to *act* according to such principles. Again, the *eudaimonic* life is one that is actually *lived* a certain way, not one that is simply dissected philosophically and abstractly as some sort of hypothetical life.[2]

---

of Plato's *Statesman* whose command of first principles "gives him an adaptability . . . such as can never be obtained by mere chapter-and-verse booklearning, but is to be compared rather to the art of the physician, because it arises from living and productive knowledge". W. Jaeger, *Aristotle*, p. 262.

2. As Henry Veatch so felicitously puts it, "So, for Aristotle, the final cause of human existence, the achievement of the good life or the intelligent life, is not merely a matter of right knowledge or know-how—although it is at least that. But it is also a matter of right desire and of choosing the right, and choosing it for its own sake." Henry B. Veatch, *Aristotle: A Contemporary Appreciation*, p. 108. In this same vein, K. von Fritz and E. Kapp

TABLE 1
Table of Virtues

VICE *(Excess)*	VICE *(Deficiency)*	VIRTUE
Irascibility	Lack of Feeling	Gentleness
Foolhardiness	Cowardice	Bravery
Shamelessness	Shyness	Modesty
Intemperance	Insensibility	Temperance
Envy	(Unnamed)*	Righteous indignation
Loss	Gain	The Just
Lavishness	Meanness	Liberality
Boastfulness	Self-Depreciation	Sincerity
Flattery	Surliness	Friendliness
Servility	Stubbornness	Dignity
Luxuriousness	Submission to evils	Endurance
Vanity	Smallness of spirit	Greatness of spirit
Extravagance	Pettiness	Magnificence
Rascality	Simplicity	Wisdom

*But called *epichairekakia* in the *Nicomachean Ethics* (1108^b 2) and indicating a dispo-sition to rejoice over the bad fortune of others. It opposes envy *(phthonos)*, which is anger over the good fortune of others. Moreover, it would seem that the object of envy is one who actually deserves his good fortune, and the object of *epichairekakia* is one who does not deserve his bad fortune. The virtue of righteous indignation, after all, is one in which anger is aroused by good fortune visiting the underserving.

Such a life is not possible for a person lacking in *phronesis*, but practical wisdom alone is not enough. A man may know what the virtuous course of action is, but still not follow it. He may confuse *eudaimonia* with mere pleasure, or be pulled away from intellec-tualized principles by uncontrolled appetites. He may just be more responsive to the call of passion than the voice of reason. If this is to be averted, the very character of a man must be *made* better, for the dispositions in question do not arise spontaneously or by instinct.

But it is difficult to get from youth up a right training for excel-lence if one has not been brought up under right laws; for to live temperately and hardily is not pleasant to most people, espe-

have written that, "Aristotle's words leave no doubt that in the field of political science, just as in medicine, one has to be an 'expert' first, before one can make appropriate use of the written material . . . the study of books . . . will *not* make an expert." K. von Fritz and E. Kapp, "The Development of Aristotle's Political Philosophy and the Concept of Nature," in Barnes, Schofield, and Sorabji, eds., *Articles on Aristotle*, 2:121.

cially when they are young. For this reason, their nurture and occupations should be fixed by law ... [and] since they must, even when they are grown up, practice and be habituated to them, we shall need laws for this as well, and generally speaking to cover the whole of life; for most people obey necessity rather than argument, and punishments rather then what is noble. (*Nicomachean Ethics* 1179^b 32–1180^a 5)

It becomes clear then that, although Aristotle's Psychology of the *self* is substantialist, his Psychology of the *person* is constructivist. There is, indeed, an irreducible *self* in this theory, with self-realizing potentialities and self-interests. There is a creature of appetite and will, passion and perception. Nor is this creature a *tabula nuda* even at birth, for it is possessed of the natural, biological impulses and propensities that all complex forms of animal life bring to the external world. It is because of this that the burning question has to do with the extent to which the animalistic will prevail; the extent to which the potentiality for the *eudaimonic life* will be realized in a creature that is at once rational and animal. The Socratic dialogues are often silent, when not disdainful, on the animalistic side of human nature. Aristotle is ever prepared to consider it and to acknowledge its importance and its naturalness.[3] Like Plato, he will look for the answer to the burning question in the social context in general and in the governing political climate especially. But unlike the Socratics, he will not find the answer personified in the Moral Hero, the wise man who might as well be an extraterrestrial. Indeed, the *Politics* is informed by Aristotle's careful analysis of more than 150 constitutions and by his extraordinary and surviving analysis of *The Constitution of Athens*. His political *science*, then, is naturalistic and empiricistic. He does not ignore the facts of shifting political fortunes, nor does he assert the primacy of any theory or logical canon over these. For Aristotle, the flourishing life is lived within a community by beings who are by nature social, and within a state whose aims and purposes are sensitive to this nature and capable of nurturing it. This flourishimg life is not to be confused with merely outward appearances of prosperity, nor is the activity of the *eudaimonic* state exclusively or even primarily outward. It is the inner prosperity of the mind that

3. An enlightening discussion of what distinguishes Aristotle's teaching from the Socratics on this point is provided by Martha Nussbaum, "Shame, Separateness, and Political Unity: Aristotle's Criticism of Plato" (ch. 21), in Rorty, ed., *Essays on Aristotle's Ethics*.

disposes one's outward actions. The man of honor has honor within himself (*Politics* 1325^b 14–32). But he is a social being nonetheless, and his nature cannot be fully realized except within the *polis*. The thesis is advanced with arresting clarity in the *Politics*[4]:

> A social instinct is implanted in all men by nature, and yet he who first founded the state was the greatest of benefactors. For man, when perfected, is the best of animals, but, when separated from law and justice, he is the worst of all; since armed injustice is the more dangerous, and he is equipped at birth with arms, meant to be used by intelligence and excellence, which he may use for the worst ends. (1253^a 30–36)

Even relationships of lesser scope than that between citizen and government come to shape and to express the moral qualities of the participants. The relationship of friendship is illustrative of Aristotle's entire theory of social relationships and serves as an informing introduction to the theory. Friendship reveals in an intimate and simplified form the principal (or, alas, unprincipled) grounds of affiliation that operate at the level of citizenship and statesmanship as well.

There are, says Aristotle, as many kinds of friendship as there are reasons for loving or attributes that make things lovable; either for the pleasure the object produces, or for the uses to which it can be put, or for what it is in and of itself. But to love something for its utility or for the pleasure it produces is finally a species of *self-love* since the criterion that has to be satisfied is solely what is desired by the lover. To this extent, the object of love may be regarded merely as an object, valueless except for the premium others are prepared to place on it.[5] Moreover, usefulness and pleasure are both ephemeral and so too, therefore, must be the love that is aroused by and attached to them. Perfect friendship *(teleia philia)* cannot be based on such considerations (*Nicomachean Eth-*

4. Werner Jaeger in his *Aristotle* pp. 260–263) records his skepticism regarding the ordering of the eight books of the *Politics*, and recounts several of the influences behind the various versions of the work assembled over the centuries. Here, as elsewhere, Professor Jaeger's genetic theory finds the older Aristotle condemning Platonic theories to which earlier he had subscribed.

5. As Professor Nussbaum shows, this subjective standard of value is endorsed by John Rawls in his treatment of self-respect and shame, whereas Aristotle gives them objective value. She says that on the Rawlsian account, "a position that is not felt as shameful is not so. And if you *feel* your life plan to be a worthy one and *feel* confident that you can carry it out, that appears sufficient to make you a person of self-respect" ("Shame, Separateness, and Political Unity," p. 398). Professor Rawls' thesis is found in his *A Theory of Justice*, especially pp. 29, 67.

ics 1156ᵃ 6–1156ᵇ 6). A perfect friendship is abiding. One obstacle to it is the triumph over reason of just those appetites or emotions on which hedonistic and utilitarian considerations are based. Where these are dispository, judgment and rational choice are not.

With perfect friendship, however, there is the relationship between persons who are both good, both similar in virtue. Such persons "wish well alike to each other qua good, and they are good in themselves" (*Nicomacheon Ethics* 1156ᵇ 7–10). Their relationship endures, for the bond itself (which is *arete*) is an enduring one. But so too is it rare, for the qualities of such friends are rare.

Note that the other aims of friendship—utility and pleasure—imply nothing about the character of those involved. Evil persons can and do use each other for personal advantage, and vicious persons can and do derive pleasures from their associations. With true friendship, what is loved is that which is worthy of love in and of itself, its value not contingent on the whims or tastes of others. Friendship is not just an expression of love, however, for one can bestow this sentiment on beautiful but lifeless things, or on others who do not share the affection. Love, then, is a passion or emotion *(pathos)* that does not entail reciprocation and that is not even limited to living recipients. Friendship, however, is an enduring condition *(hexis)* that is reciprocated on the basis of principled choices *(prohaireseis)* made by each of the friends (1157ᵇ 25–32). Friendship, as a bond requiring choice and judgments of worthiness, is a state that expresses the moral worth of those who have entered into it. One cannot be blamed for one's parents or one's children, though one can be blamed for one's friends.

Both true love and perfect friendship are exceedingly rare. They are similar in that each results from the uniquely compatible chemistry that enters into the relationship. The parties, in addition to having feelings of respect and affection, receive pleasure from each other and may also be useful to one another. Pleasure and utility, it should be noted, are not only permissible but typical aspects of principled relationships which involve, after all, human beings with desires and needs. They are not, however, the ultimate goal or the identifying feature of perfect friendship, as they are in commoner relationships; e.g., those involving "commercially minded" people (1158ᵃ 21–22). In the perfect friendship obtaining between persons of excellent character, the friends look for and find the same things in each other, which is why such friendships are possible only between equals. As equals, the friends represent and are what is worthy of love in and of itself. As persons of excellent character, it is just this that they are disposed to love. So each supplies what the other desires. If, therefore, one of them is a man of virtue, the other would have to be equally virtuous or would not be able to provide what a virtuous person desires. Each of them desires good for the other and for the other's own sake.

Of course, imperfect friendships, friendships based on utility or pleasure, are also entered into by equals. To establish that A and B are equal is not to show that both are excellent. Both might be morally defective, but equally so. Equality is necessary but not sufficient for principled friendship, the "friendship of excellence" (1158^b 12).

There are forms of friendship in which the participants are not equal, such as those between father and children, husband and wife, ruler and subject. Before considering Aristotle's (infamous) theories about slaves and women, it is important to acknowledge the systematic nature and the coherence of his theory of friendship. *If* it is the case that neither child nor woman nor slave is the equal of a man of excellent character, *then* it follows that the latter will not find as much to love in them as they will find in him.

> Each party, then, neither gets the same from the other, nor ought to seek it. . . . In all friendships implying inequality the love also should be proportional, i.e., the better should be more loved than he loves, and so should the more useful, and similarly in each of the other cases; for when the love is in proportion to the merit of the parties, then in a sense arises equality, which is held to be characteristic of friendship. (*Nicomachean Ethics* 1158^b 19–28)

It is clear from this account that, even among the manifestly unequal, the possibility of friendship exists if there is at least *equal justice*, here taken to be a meritocratic calculus for giving and receiving love itself (1162^a 34–1162^b 4). What preserves equal justice in such relationships is the commitment to a principle of distribution based on earned deserts. This is no accident, for Aristotle regards friendship and justice as being concerned with the same objectives and involving the same persons. Thus, in government as in friendship, the person who has nothing of value to contribute to others receives no honor, whereas those who provide great benefits for others are revered (*Nicomachean Ethics* 1163^b 5–

12). The general conclusion reached through these deliberations is this:

> To kinsmen, too, and fellow-tribesmen and fellow citizens and to every other class one should always try to assign what is appropriate, and to compare the claims of each class with respect to nearness of relation and to excellence or usefulness. (1165ᵃ 30–33)

Whether one is dealing with one's father or one's subjects or wife or children or (equal or unequal) friends and acquaintances, there is a proper measure of love, respect, or recompense to be paid and to be received. The rule of reason finds and sets the level, even where no more than utility is at stake. Persons at the level of friendship are akin to citizens within a constitutional order. Their expectations and duties, both legal and moral, should be based upon their contributions to the good of the whole, and (where persons of excellence are concerned) the contribution of their goodness to the goodness of the whole. But in this, one's stripes are earned every day, for a good man can become evil and thus no longer be worthy of friendship (1165ᵇ 13–23). And, as will be seen, he is no longer worthy of citizenship, either.

A meritocratic system of distribution need not be political or familial. It might be merely commercial, as in contexts in which piecework wages vary according to the productivity of the worker. Within the political context, however, merit must have some defining form. How, then, are one's merits to be assessed within the political context? Are all merits within this context worthy of equal consideration and, therefore, reward? Aristotle addresses these questions in Book III of his *Politics*, noting that honors and powers should be generically tied to the particular objectives of that enterprise within which praise and blame are bestowed. It would be a mistake, he says, to reward with the best flutes those flute players who are the best born or have the best complexions. If the prize is to be the finest flute, then the proper recipient should be the best flute player, since the whole point of the reward is to advance the art of music (*Politics* 1282ᵇ 27–1283ᵃ 2). Those excellences that are to be held as worthy of influence within the state and of rewards from it must be based upon what turns out to be the whole point of the state. What, then, is a state *(polis)*, what are its ends and what is the nature of the relationship between the individual citizen and this collective?

If answers to such questions are to be free of postclassical theories of government—including those that are putatively in the "aristotelian" tradition—it is necessary at the outset to recognize that, for Aristotle, the *polis* is a *natural* phenomenon. It is not something produced for *ad hoc* purposes, nor is it but one of an indefinitely large number of possible social entities. The human *erga* for which the state provides are themselves natural to human beings and proceed from nothing less than human nature itself. It is because "man is by nature a political animal" that the *polis* "is a creation of nature" (*Politics* 1253ª 3–4). But as with other natural phenomena, the state reaches its mature expression only after a period of evolutionary development.

For there to be a *polis* there must, of course, be people, and this requires a natural tendency to procreate. The procreative union of man and woman is instinctual, as it is with "other animals and plants," and is "not of choice" (*Politics* 1252ª 25–31). The impulse to sexual union is in response to *orexeis*, not *prohaireseis*, and the purpose served is that of the survival of the species. The same factors lead to familial affiliations and to tribal villages governed by elders in the manner of royal rule. When a number of such villages combine to form a self-sufficient community, a state has been established, "originating in the bare needs of life, and continuing in existence for the sake of a good life. And therefore, if the earlier forms of society are natural, so is the state, for it is the end of them, and the nature of a thing is its end. For what each thing is when fully developed, we call its nature, whether we are speaking of a man, a horse, or a family" (*Politics* 1252ᵇ 28–1253ª 1).

Aristotle goes on to make the surprising claim that the state is not only natural, but that it is *prior to the family and to the individual* (1253ª 19). His reasoning here proceeds from the scientific and metaphysical theories reviewed in chapter 3. The final cause of anything predates the thing itself; e.g., the plan to create a silver bowl comes before the bowl. The *that for the sake of which* is the completed form of the thing and is thus its cause, and causes come before their effects. It is in this sense that the living and properly functioning body is aetiologically prior to hands and feet and hair, etc., for "if the whole body be destroyed, there will be no foot or hand, except homonymously, as we might speak of a stone hand; for when destroyed the hand will be no better than that. . . . [T]hings are defined by their function and power; and we ought not to say that they are the same when they no longer have their proper quality" (*Politics* 1253ª 20–24).

Things are defined by their *ergon* and their *dunamis*. Man is by nature a political and social animal. The man separated from society and without a political community, says Aristotle, is Homer's "tribeless, lawless, hearthless one," comparable to "an isolated piece at draughts" (1253ª 4–6). Detached from the state, man is not self-sufficient and is not able to realize his defining task or mission, his *idion ergon*. It is through the state that human character can be perfected; it is in the absence of this that the human character remains unformed and deformed.

A political community has rulers and subjects, a fact that is as reasonable as it is common. It is paralleled by that duality of body and of soul, where the soul is intended to be the ruling principle, the body its instrument. That this is the intended relationship can be established rationally, but it is also evident in those who have in fact perfected both their physical and their psychic powers. In all such persons, it is the realm of deliberation and reason that commands the body and not *vice versa* (1254ª 20–38). In the state, too, there must be a ruling principle to which the populace is obedient if the very ends for which the state exists are to be realized.

It is here that what might be called Aristotle's "Psychology of individual differences" is introduced as an argument for slavery and for political dominance by men and subservience by women. Certainly no one writing at the end of the twentieth century is under any obligation to defend either Aristotle's argument or the conclusions it yields. There is, however, an obligation to understand it.[6] It is useful to state it in Aristotle's own words:

> The male is by nature superior, and the female inferior; and the one rules, and the other is ruled; this principle, of necessity, extends to all mankind. Where then there is such a difference as that between soul and body, or between men and animals (as in the case of those whose business is to use their body and who can do nothing better), the lower sort are by nature slaves, and it is

6. Not surprisingly, the most recent decade has witnessed a spate of critical commentary on the "racist" and "sexist" character of the classical age, with both Plato and Aristotle treated to special rebukes. A thoughtful essay on the central issues is W. W. Fortenbaugh, "Aristotle on Slaves and Women," in Barnes et al., eds., *Articles on Aristotle*, vol. 2, ch. 12.

better for them as for all inferiors that they should be under the rule of a master. For he who can be, and therefore is, another's, and he who participates in reason enough to apprehend, but not to have, is a slave by nature. Whereas the lower animals cannot even apprehend reason; they obey their passions. (1254^b 12–23)

This is, to say the least, not an equivocal position. As W. W. Fortenbaugh has written, however, it is also neither "psychologically foolish nor morally repulsive."[7] Aristotle regards it as factual that persons are born with different physical and psychological endowments. The great differences obtaining among the distinguishable species of animals can be seen in much smaller degree between members of the same species. There are visible physical differences, less visible but far more consequential psychological differences.[8] The chief distinction between human animals and lower animals is the human capacity to conform conduct to the dictates of reason, with reason ruling over the emotional and appetitional motives. Even the natural slave can be reasoned with, though lacking in the powers conferred by reason. But in the absence of reasons supplied by his superiors, the natural slave would be unable to regulate his own conduct except according to animalistic principles.

Slavery as Aristotle actually observed it was the product of warfare, the losing side forfeiting liberty and honor in favor of (mere) life. Slaves of this sort are slaves by convention and not "natural" slaves. Aristotle specifically rejects the proposition that the more powerful have either a moral or an intellectual superiority over the vanquished (1255^a 4–10). Indeed, the abuse of power by a master is wrong. There are conditions and circumstances calling for the relationship of master and slave, though such pragmatic considerations need not preclude even a kind of friendship based on common interests (1255^b 10–15).

The natural slave, therefore, is a creature able to comprehend the rational counsel of others but unable to frame a reasonable and principled *curriculum vitae* for himself. His limitations are not those imposed by a more powerful adversary but those arising

7. "Aristotle on Slaves and Women," p. 137. It is not psychologically foolish because there are, in fact, instances in which the mentally defective must rely on the solicitude of others and be totally obedient to their sound counsel. It is not morally repulsive, for *if there are such individuals*, there is a duty to control their activities.
8. At 1254^b 38–39, he remarks that the beauty of the body is seen, that of the soul, invisible. But the justification of superior rank is implicit in those of superior *psyche*.

from an inner deficiency and, presumably, an innate one. The term "slave" *(doulos)* is, of course harsh and refers to a deplorable chapter in social history. But Aristotle does not use it with condescension or arrogance. His discussions of the "natural slave" are no different from his descriptions of other natural phenomena. An entity is a slave by nature when, by its very nature, it lacks the means by which to live the life available to free human beings—a life in which one's significant actions and relationships proceed from principled choices grounded in reason. A creature lacking a fully developed rational power, or one in whom passion rules in an abiding way is not free. Transitory forms of such a state can be produced by drunkenness or injury or illness. But a permanent state of this sort—one typically dating from birth—is a state of natural slavery, pure and simple. That the victim should be the possession of another, if only in the sense of protective custody, is a proposition that is "neither psychologically foolish nor morally repulsive."

The issue of gender differences, which would appear to be entirely different from that of slavery, actually arises from similar, though more subtle, considerations. For Aristotle the biologist and psychologist, the program of natural science calls for reliable and defensible standards of classification into species and genera. In Book x of *Metaphysics*, he considers the question as to the basis on which men and women (and male and female in general) can be members of the same species even though the differences are innate and profound. He says this:

> This question is almost the same as the other, why one contrariety makes things different in species and another does not, e.g., "with feet" and "with wings" do, but whiteness and blackness do not. Perhaps it is because the former are modifications peculiar to the genus, and the latter are less so. . . . [M]ale and female are indeed modifications peculiar to animal, not however in virtue of its substance but in the matter, i.e., the body. (1058ᵃ 29–1058ᵇ 23)

Clearly, Aristotle rejects the proposition that men and women are different types of substance. Such inferiorities as might befall the female members of the species are largely biological in origin, but no less important for this reason. Biologically, the female is disposed toward passivity, the male, activity. He has found evidence for this in many places; e.g., in reproduction, the male contributes semen but female contributes only a substance that this

123

semen can act upon (*Generation of Animals* 729ᵃ 21–33). In his
History of Animals, the most general form of the theory is advanced:

> In all genera in which the distinction of male and female is found,
> nature makes a similar differentiation in the characteristics of
> the two sexes. This differentiation is the most obvious in the case
> of human kind and in that of the larger animals and the vivipa-
> rous quadrupeds. For the female is softer in character, is the
> sooner tamed, admits more readily of carressing, is more apt in
> the way of learning. . . . The fact is, the nature of man is the most
> rounded off and complete, and consequently in man the qualities
> above referred to are found most clearly. Hence woman is more
> compassionate than man, more easily moved to tears, at the
> same time is more jealous, more querulous, more apt to scold
> and to strike. She is, furthermore, more prone to despondency
> and less hopeful than the man, more void of shame, more false of
> speech, more deceptive, and of more retentive memory. She is
> also more wakeful, more shrinking, more difficult to rouse to
> action, and requires a smaller quantity of nutriment. (*History of
> Animals* 608ᵃ 19–608ᵇ 13)

On the assumption that the last of these attributes was not
inserted for purposes of whimsy, Aristotle must be understood here
as providing a classificatory sketch of those gender-differences that
mark out both the physical and the temperamental *differentiae*
common among the species. What is important to establish is that
these characterizations are intended to be part of the "natural
science" of his psychology and, as such, are grounded in his own
observations and those related to him from other sources. Equally
important is the fact that these characterizations are generalities
—as are all of his naturalistic conclusions—admitting of exceptions and of more than one interpretation. As in the instance of his
theory of the natural slave, so too in this instance the political
program as regards men and women is reasonable *if the natural
science is sound.* Obviously, if there really is no one answering to
the profile developed for the natural slave, then Aristotle's *polis*
will have no such entities in it. And if the psychobiological attributes of females are just different from what Aristotle has asserted,
then the role he would give to women in relation to men no longer
is valid.

In anchoring the structure and operations of the *polis* to those
scientific principles and facts unearthed in his naturalistic studies,

Aristotle produces a society unacceptable to modern, liberal, and "liberated" sensibilities. Again, there is no need to defend or, for that matter, to defame what he has proposed, and even less of a reason to search for darker motives. He reached the conclusion, based on the same sort of evidence that supports all of his ethological and biological works, that women *naturally* tend to be more beholden to their emotions, less obedient to the summons of reason. It is on this basis that their status within the *polis* is determined, as it would be for any other citizen operating under the same natural inclinations and native tendencies.

In these and in all related respects, Aristotle's *polis* is radically different from Plato's republic. The latter is a product of theory to be presided over by that most improbable of eccentrics, the Philosopher-King. There is to be no private property held by the guardians of this utopian world, nor is there a place for families and their children. Ownership and competition and concern for material things all corrupt the soul and militate against the cardinal virtues (wisdom, temperance, courage, justice). Aristotle's *polis* is carved out of actually existing states, actually existing constitutional principles. He knows (or believes he knows) what conduces to citizenship and virtuous actions; he knows that men not only expect their just deserts but, alas, deserve them, and such deserts are not confined to intangibles. He knows, too, that character is *made*, not always found, that it is made through *activity*, not homilies. The mission of the state is to demand the right sort of activity and reward it and discourage the wrong sort by punishing it. It is to be the very emblem of rationality, and it accomplishes this through a devotion to principles of justice as these are implemented by good laws.

> In all sciences and arts the end is the good, and the greatest good and in the highest degree a good in the most authoritative of all —this is the political science of which the good is justice, in other words, the common interest. (*Politics* 1282^b 14–16)

As in the *Republic*, so too in Aristotle's *polis*, careful attention is given to the conditions of nurturance surrounding the moral education of children. Interestingly, Book VIII of *Politics* has long passages devoted to music, whose themes and melodies are able to create the full range of emotions and "supply imitations of anger and gentleness, and also of courage and temperance" (1340^a 19–20). In contrast with Socrates, however, Aristotle argues that cultural forms, too, are to vary with the stages and seasons of life and must take cognizance of the special needs and powers of their patrons. Education *(paideia)* must, therefore, always acknowledge the principles of the mean *(meson)*, of the possible *(dunaton)* and of becoming *(prepon)*, each of these varying to some degree according to the developmental state attained by the citizen (1342^b 19–34).

The forms of government in their way reflect the forms of character expressed by individuals who are at once rational, passionate, self-interested, and willful. Aristotle finds tendencies toward one or another form of vice in each form of government depending on its animating principle. He rejects the Socratic fatalistic theory according to which even the perfect state disappears because nothing is abiding (1316^a 1–14). Rather, there are definite causes of revolution and change and these can be discovered through the study of political history. Democracies, for example, tend to be undone by the intemperance of demagogues who appeal to the masses, often by assailing the prosperous (1304^b 21–24). With oligarchies, unrest arises through the jealousies of the leaders; in aristocracies, through a failure to reward excellence outside the ruling circle. On the whole, any form of government can succeed if it is well balanced and if within it nothing is "more jealously maintained than the spirit of obedience to law" (1307^b 31–32). It is the *rational* principle that must rule, and the appetites and emotions that must obey.

Forms of government must be shaped to the particular circumstances and characters of the governed. Many of the defects of democracy, for example, are circumvented in an agricultural state. Here the people work away at the necessities of life, have little time for political intrigues and ambitions, prefer life on the land to that within the bureaucracy, and are content to be able to put their magistrates on notice (1318^b 7–16). For the most part, the judgment reached about the aptness of a given form of government must be based upon historical and demographic factors and, in any case, is not entirely deducible from the armchair. All of the principled forms of government are able to strive for that end which justifies government itself and explains its origins. It is more correct, therefore, to consider the functions than the types of political organization. Or, setting matters of structure aside, it is more correct to say that the best form of government is that in which persons are at their best and act their best and live in happiness (1324^a 22–23).

This is all to the good for those who are thus governed, but there remains a problem for the statesman and for the man of excellence in general. The life of political activity devoted to creating and maintaining this republic of virtue would seem to leave no room for the life of philosophical reflection. Which of these lives is better? In his *Politics*, Aristotle sees this as a vexing question, but remains hopeful that the wise man—in either office—will act according to the best end (1324ª 29–35). The best end of man and for the state is the same end, which is one of harmony and justice. For the state, there is the goal of security and prosperity at home, justice within and peace with neighbors. The state achieves its end when it has made citizens good and has put them on the path of a flourishing life. The individual achieves his end when he has contributed to the efforts of the *polis* and has thereby come to live a kind of life only possible within a just and ordered community. The question still remains, however, as to the essential tone and character of that life which, even at a distance, seems nearly divine.

NINE

Transcendence and Sublimity

A casual reading of Aristotle's surviving ethical and political works might encourage the conclusion that the individual person for him was but a cog in the larger machinery of statecraft, to be praised or rebuked by other citizens depending on his contribution to the whole. As noted earlier, the virtues discussed at length by Aristotle are social in nature and in effect, and even these must be understood according to prevailing cultural circumstances and the ethical norms bequeathed by tradition. The *self* seems lost in the analysis, and the vaunted state of *eudaimonia* too often comes across as a prosperous duchy of good manners, quiet strength, and cultivated taste.

Then, too, the ethical and political treatises are likely to earn the skepticism, if not the contempt, of an age that prides itself on egalitarian principles and a liberal disposition toward the right of individuals to define their own terms of happiness and to pursue this happiness unhindered by the heavy hand of bureaucracy. The Aristotle of the *Politics*, with his theory of the natural slave, his depiction of democracies as a "deviant" species—rule by a majority that is poor, the way oligarchies are rule by a minority that is rich—his outrageous characterizations of women, must seem at first glance to be as remote as his epoch. Moreover, he must seem also to be estranged from that other Aristotle, the observant naturalist armed with a thousand enchanting stories about exotic species and their strange instincts. All in all, the *Politics* is an uneven work, probably incomplete and perhaps too hastily composed in a number of places.[1] Its concluding books (vii and viii) seek to characterize the ideal state *(ariste politeia)*, but the demographic and social assumptions are now so beyond the realm of possibility that the entire analysis appears hopelessly utopian in the least attractive sense of the term. It is, of course, a "realistic" analysis in comparison with Plato's *Republic*, if only because it is informed by history and enriched by the author's genius for observation and classification. Nonetheless, at least on its surface, it is a treatise that ends in midstream.

Beneath the surface, however, the *Politics* is a poignant essay, written in Athens by a man who was, alas, not an Athenian, and written at a time when, it might be surmised, the political horizon was less than comforting.[2] His reference to the stateless man in Homer who is "tribeless, lawless, hearthless" records Aristotle's own deep and philosophically reasoned conviction that human life as such is a rootless and fragile affair, luckless and bereft of direction when cut off from a worthy and caring society of one's equals and one's betters. The *Politics*, long recognized as Aristotle's completion of his project in ethics, is also a study in what its author tends to regard as man's last hope. Plato longed for the Philosopher-King. Aristotle understands that a more abiding influence is needed; one that can enjoy a continuing history, a continuing influence down through the ages. Plato's republic is remote where Aristotle's *ariste politeia* is at least sublunary. A state grounded in *constitutional* principles can outlive the tempests of the moment, the Heraclitean forces that shatter the merely material world. A human life grounded in principles has the same hopeful prospects.

1. In his *Aristotle*, Sir David Ross begins his discussion of the *Politics* with the usual caveat; i.e., that the work "presents a difficult and much-discussed problem" (p. 235). Werner Jaeger's *Aristotle* devotes pages to establishing the problematic of the order of the text and its relation to Aristotle's own development as a theorist.

2. Aristotle mentions within the work the death of Philip of Macedon (336 B.C.), which would seem to provide the earliest date of composition though, as noted, the current version of the work may be less complete than the original. The death of Philip could be seen as marking a promising turn in Aristotle's own fortunes in light of his earlier relationship with Alexander. If, however, due credit is given to Aristotle's uncommon perspicacity, he must have envisaged among the several possibilities the utterly non-Athenian political reality that Alexander finally did bring about.

Each needs the other, realizes the potential of the other, authenticates the other.

In Book x of the *Nicomachean Ethics*, Aristotle is found again wrestling with the tension between the life of action and the life of contemplation. "If happiness is activity in accordance with excellence, it is reasonable that it should be in accordance with the highest excellence; and this will be that of the best thing in us" (1177ᵃ 11–13). He must follow the very logic of the argument that he has developed in all of his naturalistic writings; the logic that identifies the essence of a thing with its purpose, and its purpose with its defining powers. Whatever turns out to be "the best thing in us," "the activity of this in accordance with its proper excellence will be complete happiness. That this activity is contemplative we have already said" (1177ᵃ 16–18).

By "contemplative" *(theoretikos)*, Aristotle has more in mind than self-absorption. The Greek word is rooted in meanings that include the observant spectator, not only the speculator. The *theoretic* life, then, is a life of self-improvement through systematic study of consequential matters. Politics and generalship are lacking in leisure and have ulterior aims. Wisdom is courted for itself:

> For while a wise man, as well as a just man and the rest, needs the necessaries of life, when they are sufficiently equipped with things of that sort the just man needs people towards whom and with whom he shall act justly, and the temperate man, the brave man, and each of the others is in the same case, but the wise man, even when by himself, can contemplate truth. . . . And this activity alone would seem to be loved for its own sake. (1177ᵃ 28–1177ᵇ 2)

As Martha Nussbaum has observed,[3] Plato's theory of the person gives the soul so disembodied an existence as to remove it from life as it is actually lived by persons. Aristotle, ever the commonsense naturalist, takes man as he finds him, discovers a precious and unprecedented power, and then strives to discover the means by which this rarest faculty might flourish *even as the rest of the person flourishes as well.* But a conflict between the interests of rational man and those of sensitive, emotional, and passionate man cannot be precluded indefinitely. It would require nothing less than the Ideal State to provide such safeguards, and this is something real-

3. Nussbaum, "Shame, Separataeness, and Political Unity," 412 ff.

ists hope for but do not expect. Only one life can survive the collisions intact, and that is the contemplative life.[4]

These conclusions in place, Aristotle must then face the astounding implications. Consider only what has been established to this point in the argument—to this point in his entire anthropological program: 1) Man is a creature of nature, fitted out by nature to procreate, to serve the needs of his body, to defend himself against attack, to combine with others for mutual defense. 2) The appetites and passions of human beings, like those found throughout the more complex reaches of the animal kingdom, are intimately associated with survival, defense, affiliation, pleasure, utility. 3) Man also possesses a form of intellectual power permitting abstract thought and deliberated choice. Together, these yield a moral side to human life and allow human beings to live according to the precepts of law within a political community. This, too, is the culmination of an entirely natural process, though one tied exclusively to *human* nature. 4) Yet, with all of this duly noted, the very exercise of this special power—the very immersion in the life of the mind—yields pleasures sweeter than all the rest and might even proceed within that theater of the macabre and the absurd routinely served up by history's villains. What is to be said about a life capable of finding not only happiness but the most excellent form of happiness in an activity that holds out nothing beyond the activity itself?

> Such a life would be too high for man; for it is not in so far as he is man that he will live so, but in so far as something divine is present in him; and by so much as this is superior to our composite nature is its activity superior to that which is the exercise of the other kind of excellence. If intellect is divine, then, in comparison with man, the life according to it is divine in comparison with human life. (1177[b] 27–31)

The biologist has run his argument to the end of its empirical and taxonomic tethers and now discovers in this creature of nature something that transcends the natural order. Even the ethicist must be perplexed, for the greatest happiness of this creature turns

4. Amélie O. Rorty puts it this way: "When they (the theoretic and the practical lives) conflict, the palms are given to the contemplative life, because the independence of the intellectual from the moral virtues allows contemplation to continue in the midst of political disaster and practical blindness" (p. 392). Amélie O. Rorty, "The Place of Contemplation in Aristotle's *Nicomachean Ethics*," in Rorty, ed., *Essays on Aristotle's Ethics.*

out to be aloof even to that social and political world in which ethical prescriptions operate. The moral excellences are tied to the passions and appetites and arise from man's *composite nature*. But this promised ultimate condition of happiness is not part of this at all. It thus becomes clearer why Aristotle would qualify the essence of Homer's stateless man—one who is stateless *by nature*—as that of a man who is "either a bad man, *or above humanity*" (*Politics* 1253^b 3, emphasis added). To find the divine within oneself, if only for the moment, is to be stateless and, indeed, lawless and hearthless as well. The moment of sublimity has no social features, no tribal customs, no locale. Busy people might be expected not only to deny the possibility but to regard even talk about such matters as rubbish bordering on hubris. But, says Aristotle,

> we must not follow those who advise us, being men, to think of human things, and, being mortal, of mortal things, but must, so far as we can, make ourselves immortal, and strain every nerve to live in accordance with the best thing in us; for even if it be small in bulk, much more does it in power and worth surpass everything. (*Nicomachean Ethics* 1177^b 31–1178^a 1)

It is not dreamy speculation that serves as the final test of this thesis, or even (*contra* Socrates) the intuitive certainties possessed by the wise man, for "the truth in practical matters is discerned from the facts of life" (1179^a 19–20). What is clear from a study of noble and emulable lives is that the life of the mind produces the best state that man can occupy, and one that is most dear to the gods as well, for it is a life most like their own (1179^a 20–29).

In the fragmentary *Protrepticus*,[5] the same theme is sounded again and again, in passages of moving simplicity. The end of a thing is better than the thing itself, and in that duality of human nature—body and soul—the development and the excellence of the former is designed for the use of the latter. Within the realm of *psyche* itself, it is the rational power that is last to appear and that comes to direct the operations of all the rest. It is, then, the culmination of human development and, therefore, the *that for the sake of which* all other powers and functions exist. The proof that the

5. The provenance of this work remains unsettled. There may have been a full-scale treatise written when Aristotle was still in the Academy—the fragments are richly "Platonic"—or the passages may be redactions of such a work compiled by others. Whatever the source, however, the spirit of the *Protrepticus* is at one with the celebration of the contemplative life found in *Nicomachean Ethics*.

telos of human life is a contemplation of the truth is finally the fact that it is possible at all. Nature does not bestow such powers without a purpose.

Those who fail to distinguish between what is good in itself and what is merely useful or practical are guilty of a profound ignorance: "One would see the absolute truth of what we are saying if someone as it were carried us in thought to the Isles of the Blest. For there there would be need of nothing and no profit from anything: and there remains only thought and contemplation, which even now we describe as the free life."[6]

Is it the case that the basic difference between the Platonic and the Aristotelian systems is grounded in nothing less than a different attitude toward man and the world? Yes and No. The platonic *psyche* has an origin and destiny separated in principle from any earthly life with which it is but transiently connected. Earth for this *psyche* is a prison, grudgingly accepted and happily abandoned. It must come to terms with hostile powers—the senses, the emotions, willfulness, and arrogant self-assertions by the cave dweller—but it may find itself joined on occasion to one who has received the light of philosophy and is, therefore, prepared to be in but not of this world.

The Aristotelian *psyche* is a principle that operates wherever there is life. It is the driving engine of *phusis*, capable of moving entities toward their proper ends, thus fulfilling the prescriptions laid down by the very nature of things. Sensation, perception, appetite, emotion, will, reason—they all come from the mint of nature and they all have a vital and cherished part to play in the life of man. It is in the history of human development—both of the individual and of communities of individuals—that the intended plan becomes obvious; the several powers and propensities of the species must finally be subservient to its highest power, the power of reason. Any other hierarchy must lead to a dissolute life, a corrupt and corrupting *polis*. It is accountability and control among the participating elements that establish the very character of the enterprise, whether the object of concern is the person or the state. Where appetite rules and principle obeys, there is no ruling principle, only a condition of *anarcheia*. To be a person of this sort is to be a slave by nature; one who might comprehend the dictates of reason but who cannot frame them for himself and pattern his life

6. [B43], Fr. 58 R³ (*Iamblichus*, Protrepticus 52.16—54.5 *Pistelli*).

after them. "It is slave-like," says Aristotle, "to desire to live rather than to live well,"[7] but here again, to *live well* is to live free from tormenting and unrequited desires. To live well is to have what is worth having without surrendering to a lesser value. In friendship, it is to befriend one for his virtue, not his usefulness, and thus to befriend that which is good in and of itself. In solitary life, it is to befriend wisdom, for no purpose beyond the inestimable happiness that comes from a love of goodness for its own sake. The disposition to live life this way establishes yet another duality not unlike that of body and soul. It establishes an earthly life for a creature of nature that is also a life of sublimity that transcends human nature and reaches toward the gods. Like true love and perfect friendship, like the Ideal State itself, sublimity must be a rare condition even for the wisest. Yet, however so fleeting, it is an intimation of immortality and proof enough that reason is the author of the cosmos.

7. *Protrepticus*, [B 53].

TEXTUAL CITATIONS

701^a 32–701^b 1 (84)
703^a 37 (53)

Nicomachean Ethics
1010^b 13–15 (97)
1099^b 33–1100^a 5 (90)
1105^b 20–29 (86)
1108^b 2 (114)
1110^a 8–11 (101)
1110^a 11–14 (101)
1110^a 18–19 (102)
1110^b 2–3 (102)
1110^b 9–10 (102)
1110^b 17–18 (103)
1111^b 4–6 (92)
1111^b 7–10 (103)
1112^b 12–16 (104)
1113^a 32–1114^b 25 (105)
1114^a 32–1114^b 25 (105)
1114^b 20–21 (105)
1115^a 7 (106)
1115^b 24–30 (106)
1117^a 6–9 (107)
1117^a 20–21 (107)
1119^b 6–7 (84)
1139^a 19–20 (82)
1151^a 12–19 (96)
1152^a 7–9 (110)
1154^b 3–4 (109)
1156^a 6–1156^b 6 (117)
1156^b 7–10 (117)
1157^b 25–32 (117)
1158^a 21–22 (117)
1158^b 12 (118)
1158^b 19–28 (118)
1162^a 34–1162^b 4 (118)
1163^b 5–12 (118)
1165^a 30–33 (119)
1165^b 13–23 (119)
1173^b 21–26 (110)
1175^b 26 (110)
1177^a 11–13 (130)
1177^a 16–18 (130)
1177^a 28–1177^b 2 (130)
1177^b 27–31 (131)
1177^b 31–1178^a 1 (132)
1178^a 5–8 (110)
1179^a 19–20 (132)

1179^a 20–29 (132)
1179^a 35–1179^b 31 (113)
1179^b 32–1180^a 5 (115)

On Dreams
459^a 28–30 (68)
459^a 21 ()
459^b 11–24 (68)
460^b 3–5 (85)
460^b 20–21 (66)

On Memory
450^a 21 (70)
451^a 17 (73)
451^b 11 (70)
451^b 11–14 (70)
452^a 5–13 (73)
452^a 30 (71)
452^b 5–6 (71)
453^a 8–9 (71)

On The Heavens
312^a 12 (52)

On The Soul
403^a 30–403^b 1 (81)
405^b 33–406^a 1 (79)
407^b 14–19 (79)
407^b 19–26 (79)
408^b (65)
408^b 13–14 (65)
408^b 19 (65)
410^b (64)
413^b 2 (45)
414^b 1 (81)
415^b 23–26 (80)
424^a 1–15 (65)
424^a 18–23 (65)
424^a 28–29 (74)
424^b 22 (74)
425^a 14–425^b 12 (75)
426^b 9–23 (74)
426^b 15–17 (75)
427^b 7–28 (67)
427^b 8 (76)
428^a 11 (68)
429^a 5–9 (68)
429^a 18–429^b 22 (69)

429^a 31–429^b 4 (63)
430^a 20–26 (63)
431^a 15–17 (92)
432^a 1 (79, 92)
432^a 6 (62)
432^a 12–14 (92)
432^a 24 (85)
432^b 15–433^a 21 (80)
433^a 10–21 (80)
433^a 17 (83)
433^a 27–28 (82)
433^b 5–10 (82)
433^b 13–30 (82)

Parts Of Animals
640^b 36–641^a 3 (91)
645^a 17–27 (44)
645^a 26–645^b 1 (53)
656^a 24 (53)
656^b 8–27 (54)
658^a 12–16 (54)
663^b 23 (55)
663^b 28 (55)
667^a 14–17 (55)

Physics
184^b 13 (36)
194^b 10–15 (37)
194^b 15–195^b 30 (36)
195^b 12 (38)
197^b 6 (38)
198^a 31–33 (52)
198^b 1–3 (52)
199^a 30–33 (36)
199^b 15–19 (40)
199^b 27–30 (52)
199^b 28 (36)
200^a (60)
200^a 13 (40)
200^a 32–200^b 7 (41)
256^a 2 (78)
256^a 7–10 (78)
256^b 13–14 (78)
259^b 3–4 (79)
267^a 25–267^b 4 (79)

Politics
1252^a 25–31 (120)
1252^b 28–1253^a 1 (120)

1253^a 3–4 (120)
1253^a 4–6 (120)
1253^a 20–24 (121)
1253^a 30–36 (116)
1254^a 20–38 (121)
1254^b 12–23 (121–122)
1254^b 38–39 (122)
1255^a 4–10 (122)
1255^b 10–15 (122)
1282^b 14–16 (125)
1282^b 27–1283^a 2 (119)
1287^a 30–31 (86)
1307^b 31–32 (126)
1316^a 1–14 (126)
1318^b 7–16 (126)
1324^a 22–23 (126)
1324^a 29–35 (127)
1325^b 14–32 (116)
1340^a 19–20 (126)
1342^b 19–34 (126)

Posterior Analytics
70^b 10–15 (31)
70^b 10–72^a 30 (31)
71^a 1 (30)
71^a 25–30 (30)
72^b 20–25 (32)
73^b 25 (33)
74^b 5 (33)
75^a 30–35 (33)
76^b 10–30 (34)
76^b 25–30 (34)
79^a 7 (52)
85^a 25 (51)
89^b 22–24 (47)
99^b 25–30 (34)
100^a 1–10 (35)

Progression Of Animals
704^b 12–15 (61)

Protrepticus
B 53 (133)
B 58 (134)

Rhetoric
1360^b 4–17 (88)
1363^a 5–6 (88)
1369^b 34–1370^a 4 (98)

Textual Citations

1370^a 25–27 (98)
1378^a 21–22 (88)
1387^b 21–1388^b 29 (108)
1389^a (110)
1389^b 13–1390^a 23 (110)
1390^b 6–10 (110)
1408^a 16 (87)

Sense and Sensibilia
436^b 10 (45)
443^b 20–444^b 1 (72)

447^a 12–24 (66)
448^a 25–448^b 12 (66)
448^b 14–15 (66)

Topics
102^a 18–19 (82)
116^a 1–5 (93)
117^a 5–119^a 31 (93)
118^a 6–8 (93)
118^a 8–15 (94)

BIBLIOGRAPHY

Ackrill, J. L. "Aristotle on Eudiamonia." In A. O. Rorty, ed., *Essays on Aristotle's Ethics*, q.v.

Ackrill, J. L. *Aristotle the Philosopher*. Oxford: Oxford University Press, 1981.

Adam, James. *The Religious Teachers of Greece* [1908]. New Jersey: Reference Book Publishers, 1965.

Aristotle. *The Complete Works of Aristotle*. Jonathan Barnes, ed. Princeton: Princeton University Press, 1984.

Balme, D. M. *Review of Nussbaum's "De Motu Animalium." Journal of the History of Philosophy* (1982) 20:92–95.

Barnes, J. *Aristotle*. New York: Oxford University Press, 1982.

Barnes, J. *The Pre-Socratic Philosophers*. New York: Oxford University Press, 1979.

Barnes, J. *Early Greek Philosophy*. London: Penguin Books, 1987.

Barnes, J., M. Schofield, and R. Sorabji, eds. *Articles on Aristotle*. 4 vols. London: Duckworth, 1975.

Beier, K. "Smart on Sensations." In C. V. Borst, ed., *The Mind/Brain Identity Theory*. New York: St. Martin's Press, 1970.

Bremmer, Jan. *The Early Greek Concept of the Soul*. Princeton: Princeton University Press, [1983] 1987.

Burkert, W. *Greek Religion*. Translated from the German edition by John Raffan. Cambridge: Harvard University Press, 1985.

Burnet, J. "Philosophy." In R. W. Livingstone, ed., *The Legacy of Greece*. Oxford: Clarendon Press, 1921.

Bibliography

Chroust, A-H. *Aristotle: New Light on His Life and on Some of His Lost Works.* London: Routledge, Kegan Paul, 1973.

Cornford, F. M. *The Unwritten Philosophy.* Cambridge: Cambridge University Press, [1950] 1967.

Dane, N. and J. Ambrose. eds. *Greek Attitudes.* New York: Scribners, 1974.

Davidson, D. "How is Weakness of the Will Possible?" In J. Feinberg, ed., *Moral Concepts.* New York: Oxford University Press, 1969.

Dickinson, G. Lowes. *The Greek View of Life.* London: Methuen, [1896] 1932.

Diogenes Laertius. *Lives of Eminent Philosophers.* R. D. Hicks, trans. 2 vols. Loeb Classical Library, 1925.

Düring, I. "Aristotle and Plato in the Mid-Fourth Century." *Eranos* (1956) 54.

Fortenbaugh, W. "Aristotle on Slaves and Women." In J. Barnes, M. Schofield, and R. Sorabji, eds., *Articles on Aristotle,* q.v. vol. 2.

Furley, D. "Self-Movers." In A. O. Rorty, ed., *Essays on Aristotle's Ethics,* q.v.

Gomez-Lobo, A. "Aristotle's Hypotheses and the Euclidean Postulates." *Review of Metaphysics* (1977) 30:430–439.

Grene, M. *A Portrait of Aristotle.* Chicago: University of Chicago Press, 1963.

Hempel, C. *Aspects of Scientific Explanation and Other Essays in the Philosophy of Science.* New York: Free Press, 1965.

Heraclitus. *The Cosmic Fragments.* G. S. Kirk, trans. Cambridge: Cambridge University Press, 1962.

Herodotus. *The Persian Wars.* 2 vols. George Rawlinson, trans. F. R. B. Godolphin, ed. New York: Random House, 1942.

Hesiod. *The Works and Days.* 8th ed. Richmond Lattimore, trans. Ann Arbor: University of Michigan Press, 1973.

Hippocrates. "Airs, Waters, Places." In *Hippocrates,* W. H. S. Jones, trans. vol. 1. Loeb Classical Library. Cambridge: Harvard University Press, 1939.

Homer. *The Iliad.* Richmond Lattimore, trans. Chicago: University of Chicago Press, 1951.

Homer. *The Odyssey.* Richmond Lattimore, trans. New York: Harper and Row, 1965.

Hutchinson, D. S. *The Virtues of Aristotle.* London: Routledge, Kegan Paul, 1986.

Irwin, T. H. "The Metaphysical and Psychological Basis of Aristotle's Ethics." In A. O. Rorty, ed., *Essays on Aristotle's Ethics,* q.v.

Irwin, T. H. "Reason and Responsibility in Aristotle." In A. O. Rorty, ed., *Essays on Aristotle's Ethics,* q.v.

Jaeger, W. *Aristotle: Fundamentals of the History of His Development.* [1923] Oxford: Clarendon Press, 1934.

Kenny, A. *Aristotle's Theory of the Will.* New Haven: Yale University Press, 1979.

Lawson-Tancred, H. *Aristotle: De Anima.* London: Penguin Books, 1986.

Modrak, D. *Aristotle: The Power of Perception.* Chicago: University of Chicago Press, 1987.

Nilsson, M. P. *Homer and Mycenae.* London: Methuen [1933]; Philadelphia: University of Pennsylvania Press, 1972.

Nussbaum, M. *Aristotle's "De Motu Animalium".* Text with translation, commentary, and interpretive essays. Princeton: Princeton University Press, 1978.

Nussbaum, M. "Shame, Separateness, and Political Unity: Aristotle's Criticism of Plato." In A. O. Rorty, ed., *Essays on Aristotle's Ethics*, q.v.

Owens, J. *The Doctrine of Being in the Aristotelian "Metaphysics."* 2d ed. Toronto: Pontifical Institute, 1957.

Plato. *The Dialogues*. Benjamin Jowett, trans. 2 vols. New York: Randon House, 1937.

Plato. *Epistles*. Glenn Morrow, trans. Indianapolis: Bobbs Merrill, 1962.

Plutarch. *The Lives of the Noble Grecians and Romans*. John Dryden, trans. Edition of 1864. Reprinted, New York: Modern Library, 1932.

Rawls, J. *A Theory of Justice*. Cambridge: Harvard University Press, 1971.

Reid. T. *An Inquiry into the Human Mind on the Principles of Common Sense*. Edinburgh [1764].

Robinson, D. N. *An Intellectual History of Psychology*. New York: Macmillan, [1976] 1981.

Robinson, D. N. *Systems of Modern Psychology: A Critical Sketch*. New York: Columbia University Press, 1979.

Robinson, D. N. *Philosophy of Psychology*. New York: Columbia University Press, 1985.

Robinson, R. "Aristotle on Akrasia." In J. Barnes, M. Schofield, and R. Sorabji, eds., *Articles on Aristotle*, q.v. vol. 2.

Rohde, E. *Psyche*. [1898] H. B. Willis, trans. London: Harcourt, 1925.

Rorty, A. O., ed. *Essays on Aristotle's Ethics*. Berkeley: University of California Press, 1980.

Rorty, A. O. "The Place of Contemplation in Aristotle's *Nicomachean Ethics*." In A. O. Rorty, ed., *Essays on Aristotle's Ethics*, q.v.

Rosen, S. *Plato's Sophist: The Drama of Original and Image*. New Haven: Yale University Press, 1983.

Ross, D. *Aristotle*. [1923] London: Methuen, 1964.

Sorabji, R. *Aristotle on Memory*. London: Duckworth, 1972.

Sorabji, R. "Aristotle on the Role of Intellect in Virtue." In A. O. Rorty, ed., *Essays on Aristotle's Ethics*, q.v.

Taran, L. *Parmenides*. Princeton: Princeton University Press, 1965.

Torrey, H. and F. Felin. "Was Aristotle an Evolutionist?" *Quarterly Review of Biology* (1937), 12:1–18.

Thompson, D'Arcy. "Natural Science." In R. W. Livingstone, ed., *The Legacy of Greece*. Oxford: Clarendon, 1921.

Toynbee, A. "History." In R. W. Livingstone, ed., *The Legacy of Greece*. Oxford: Clarendon Press, 1921.

Vander Waerdt, P. A. "Peripatetic Soul-Division, Posidonius, and Middle Platonic Moral Psychology." *Greek, Roman, and Byzantine Studies* (1985), 26:373–394.

Veatch, H. *Aristotle: A Contemporary Appreciation*. Bloomington: Indiana University Press, 1974.

von Fritz, K. and E. Kapp. "The Development of Aristotle's Political Philosophy and the Concept of Nature." In J. Barnes, M. Schofield, and R. Sorabji, eds., *Articles on Aristotle*, q.v., vol 2.

Bibliography

Wiggins, D. "Deliberation and Practical Reason." In A. O. Rorty, ed., *Essays on Aristotle's Ethics*, q.v.

Wiggins, D. "Weakness of the Will." In A. O. Rorty, ed., *Essays on Aristotle's Ethics*, q.v.

Wiggins, D. "Weakness of the Will, Commensurability, and the Objects of Deliberation and Desire." In A. O. Rorty, ed., *Essays on Aristotle's Ethics*, q.v.

INDEX

Index

Free will, 101-10
Friendship, 116-19

Heart, and psychic functions, 53-54
Hellenism, 3, 7-8
Heraclitus, 18-19
Heroes, Age of, 1
Hesiod, 2, 6, 12, 23
Hippocrates, 45, 53
Homeric Hymns, 12
Homeric Psychology, 1-9, 11, 23-25,
    46-47
Homeridae, 1

Imagination, 68-69
Incorrigibility thesis, 19
Isomorphism, 76

Knowledge: classification of, 42-43;
    demonstrative, 30-34

Learning, 70-71
Logos doctrine, 73-74

Memory and recollection, 70-73
Motivation, 81-90
Movement, and the soul, 48-50, 78-83

Natural slaves, 121-23
Necessity, 38-42, see Accident;
    Chance

Old Comedy (Greek), 5, 16
Ontology, 34
Orphism, 9-12

Parmenides, 47
Plato: and Aristotle, 13-20, 25-28, 46-
    47; *Epistles*, 17-18; his philosophi-
    cal development, 14-18; psycholog-
    ical theories, 18-25, 46-47; and
    Socrates, 14-18
Politics, and human development,
    120-27

Potentiality, 50-51
Practical reasoning, 42
Protagoras, 18-19

Realism, 70, 74, 101
Religion (Greek), 2, 9-12, 17

Science, as theoretical, 43
Sensation and perception, 62-70; ba-
    sic principles, 65-69; compared
    with imagination, 68-69; as defin-
    ing animal life, 45; isomorphism,
    76; realist theory, 74; unity of per-
    ception, 74-75; veridicality of, 67-
    68
Sex differences, 57, 87, 123-25
Socrates: mind/body duality, 20-24;
    nativistic psychology, 20, 34; per-
    ception, 19-20; and Plato, 14-18; on
    the soul, 22-24; virtue, 21
Solon, judicial reforms, 7
Sophists, 16, 20
Soul, Aristotle's theory in summary,
    49-57, 64-65; Homeric theory, 4-5;
    Orphic theory, 10, 12; Socratic-Pla-
    tonic theory, 10-11, 18-24, 47-48
Spontaneity, 38-39

Teleology, 55-59, 97-101
Thinking, vs. perception, 62-63, 67;
    as a principle of movement, 80

Understanding, demonstrative, 30-34;
    see also Explanation
Universals, 33-36

Vices and virtues, 96, (table) 114;
    pre-Socratic understandings, 8

Wisdom, Aristotle's classification, 42
    Socratic theory, 20-21
Works and Days, 2

144